A NEW GUIDE TO BETTER FISHING

Over 200 fishing techniques
that will help you catch
more fish, more often.

By
Ralph Bashford

Published By

Otha Book Company
12009 Marwood Lane
Cincinnati, Ohio 45246

Printing History
1st Printing January, 1987

Printed in the United States of America

Library of Congress
Catalog Card Number 86-90704

ISBN 0-9617953-0-1

CONTENTS

Tactics For Taking Bass

Tactics For Taking Bass (cont'd.)

Tactics For Taking Crappie

Secrets For Taking Big Bluegill

Secrets For Taking Big Bluegill (cont'd.)

Tricks That Take Catfish

Carp By The Carload

How To Smoke Fish

IT IS A KNOWN FACT THAT 90 PERCENT OF ALL FISH ARE CAUGHT BY 10 PERCENT OF THE FISHERMEN.

THIS BOOK CAN HELP YOU BE AMONG THE 10 PERCENT THAT CATCH 90 PERCENT OF THE FISH.

RALPH W. BASHFORD

TACTICS FOR TAKING BASS

CHAPTER 1
THE EXOTIC BASS

Without much question, the bass is considered the most exotic of all fresh water fish. They are intelligent fish with a strong instinct for survival. They are the perfect predator with broad, powerful tails, keen vision, excellent hearing and outstanding ability to maneuver underwater quickly and accurately.

They can be caught with a casting rod, spincast outfit, fly rod, spinning rod or a simple cane pole. They have been taken on a wide variety of lures and baits: plastic worms, plugs, spinners, flies, pork chunks, crawfish, live minnows, earthworms, frogs, salamanders and many other baits. They will hit night or day in hot or cold weather and it doesn't matter if it is raining or if the sun is shining or whether it is windy or the water is calm. It is truly one of the gamest of our gamefish.

Sometimes bass will cruise around looking for food, other times they will lie in wait and strike their prey from ambush. However, they are not designed for a long chase. Instead, they prefer to strike instantly when their prey is within range. When a bass hits your lure at full charge, you'll know it. Their burst attacking speed is about twelve miles per hour.

Bass are found in all of the lower states plus Hawaii in addition to southern Canada, Mexico, Cuba and Puerto Rico. They can be found in creeks, rivers, lakes, bayous, backwater streams, farm ponds, swamps, in brackish waters, crystal clear water, swift streams and the back up waters behind river dams. They are very tolerant of a wide range of water conditions and water temperatures.

The bass is probably the most popular fish in America. In every area of our nation, there are dedicated fishermen who will fish for no other fish. They are exclusively and solely bass fishermen.

One of the factors that perhaps make the bass so very popular is his unpredictable nature. Although he can be taken on a wide variety of artifical lures and natural baits, there are days when the expert fisherman cannot score. He can be a baffling fish that will frustrate the best of fishermen on many occasions.

There is probably no greater fishing pleasure than the thrill of a bass striking your lure and then coaxing him into you boat. Bass are tough competitors and offer the supreme fishing challenge.

They are thoroughly unpredictable. Some days you can bring in your limit by hardly trying. Other days you won't draw a single strike. There isn't a bass fisherman that ever lived, professional or otherwise, that didn't get skunked more often than they were willing to admit. Perhaps this is what makes it such an exciting sport and keeps the millions of bass enthusiasts coming back year after year.

In the following pages we will be discussing dozens of techniques that when properly mastered can bring a lot of bass to your boat and greatly increase your pleasure in this fascinating sport.

CHAPTER 2
THE DIFFERENT BASS

There are various types of bass such as the largemouth bass, smallmouth bass and the spotted bass (also known as the Kentucky Bass). Although there are some differences between these three fish, there are more similarities than differences. They are relatives and many of their habits and characteristics are almost identical, especially their catlike tendencies when stalking prey. Their habitats often overlap and it is not unusual to take all three from the same spot on a given day.

Some of the differences are that the spotted bass can tolerate cooler and swifter water than the largemouth and the smallmouth can tolerate, even prefers, cooler and swifter water that the spotted bass.

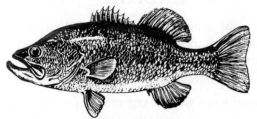

LARGEMOUTH BASS

Largemouth like weedbeds whereas the smallmouth tends to avoid them and prefers the sandy or rocky bottom of a lake or stream.

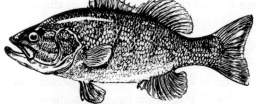

SMALLMOUTH BASS

Smallmouth spawn in cooler water than the largemouth (smallmouth in the 50's, largemouth in the 60's). All three fish tend to move to deeper waters in the fall and winter and then move into the shallow water in the spring to spawn.

The feeding habits of all three fish are very similar as are their reactions to water changes, sound, light and vibrations.

Since the three fish are so very similar in their actions and feeding habits, we will no longer refer to them as largemouth , smallmouth or spotted bass but for the most part will just use the word "bass".

Should you prefer a more detailed description of each individual fish, your public library would no doubt have larger books devoted to each fish. But since our goal will be to acquaint you with the overall habits of the bass family, we will most often use the word "bass" to cover all three.

CHAPTER 3
HABITAT

One unusual aspect of the largemouth is its ability to adapt to brackish waters (coastal waters that are part salt water and fresh water). In many of our coastal waters, you can catch largemouths right along with many ocean going fish.

The temperature which largemouth prefer is the 65 to 75 degree range. They can actually tolerate temperatures above the 75 degrees which has enabled them to adapt to the shallow lakes in the South. It has been noted that they feed more often when the water temperature is between 65 to 75. Obviously, you should make a note of that and try to be on the water when the temperature is in that range.

The original home of the largemouth bass was in marsh ponds, bayous, ox-bow lakes and slow moving rivers. However, it is such an adaptable fish and because it became so popular, it was soon introduced into wide ranging aquatic situations. In addition to the areas just mentioned, it is now found in irrigation ditches, drainage ditches, creeks, rivers, canals, reservoirs and ponds.

It is an ideal fish for stocking. It has been introduced into millions of farm ponds, natural lakes and man made lakes such as those for hydro-electric production, flood control, irrigation and water supply. It has prospered in all and now lives far outside its original range.

All bass feed primarily by sight and sound. Although they have excellent sight, they cannot open or close the iris in their eye. This forces the bass to seek shade on bright, sunny days. That is something you should want to remember. On bright days, look for bass in the shade of trees, stumps, logs or other debris.

Of course another reason that bass spend much time in shady or dark areas is that it offers a degree of protection from their enemies and at the same time it provides feeding advantages. It is far easier to remain in a semi-dark area and see prey swimming by in better-lit water. Also, it is difficult for the prey to see the bass in the darker water.

Obviously, in murky water, bass cannot see the same distance as in clear water. Instinct tells the bass that in murky waters, when prey comes within range, it is now or never. He must strike at once because once it moves beyond the range of vision, it is gone forever.

Bass can pick up the slightest vibrations of noise in the water. They can quickly and accurately detect and locate objects, such as a fishing lure, by their vibrations. Certainly the fisherman should be aware of this for it will dictate many things he should and should not do in his quest for this exotic fighter.

Bass have excellent eyesight. They have been known to strike a lure the instance it hits the water, obviously having seen it while it was still in the air. They definitely can distinguish between colors so if one color is not working on a given day, you may need to experiment to find which color is their preference for that particular occasion.

It is almost certain that bass have a keen sense of smell but it is very questionable if smell has any effect on causing a bass to strike. There are many manufacturers who have impregnated their lures with various scents and they claim it is more effective, but these statements should be taken with caution. It is a known fact that bass will seldom take dead bait that is just suspended in the water. However, give the dead bait on action, such as a pork rind, and it will draw strikes which rather strongly suggests that it is the action that draws the strikes and not the scent.

CHAPTER 4
FEEDING HABITS

Immediately at birth, the small bass fry start feeding on minute animal life in the water. As they start growing, they move up to larger prey. In the early stages, their food would consist of small insects, then move up to larger insects, small fish and eventually to crawfish, frogs and larger fish. When they reach around 7 inches in length, they will eat most anything they can swallow.

As small fry, bass are often eaten by other fish, especially the bluegill. As they grow larger, just the reverse is true and the bluegill becomes one of the favorite foods of the bass. Most every small creature you can think of has been found in the stomachs of large bass; various birds, crabs, ducklings, snakes, turtles, mice, muskrats, etc.

Feeding habits of bass can be divided into four basic areas.

One, when they are hungry and lie in ambush waiting for something large and edible to pass. During this period, they will hide in heavy cover with just the head protruding. They will remain motionless and then suddenly make a savage strike at their prey. It is during this period that you normally take your larger bass.

Two, just after feeding, bass usually move into heavy cover. With a full stomach, they like to just loll around a bit. This is normally a difficult time to entice a bass to strike. It usually depends on how long after feeding that you can expect any action. Obviously, the longer after feeding, the better will be your chances.

Third, occasionally bass like to cruise around a lake. It is assumed they are scouting for schools of forage fish. They have been studied by biologists following transistorized bass and found to travel as much as 10 miles in large reservoirs.

Fourth, bass like to frequently suspend themselves in groups. They will remain motionless at depths of 20 to 60 feet and make no effort to feed. Then, suddenly, for reasons unknown, they will disperse and move out to individual areas to their liking.

Bass are not constant eaters which is the source of much frustration for the fisherman. They have been observed to be quiet for hours with small fish swimming within easy range but they will make no effort to take them. Then, suddenly, they will strike and go on a feeding binge. Once their hunger is satisfied, they return to their contented position and will rest quietly for hours again ignoring the small fish and other creatures close by.

The favorite feeding times of bass is at dawn and dusk, however, they will almost always feed at sometime between these periods. Sometimes an approaching storm will trigger a feeding spree. Other times they will go on an eating binge when a school of shad come near.

Fortunately, bass do not always need to be hungry for you to draw a strike. We will have much to say about this a little later.

When water levels change, it often effects the feeding habits of bass but their pattern of behavior is not consistent or predictable. If a lake has been at a steady level for some time and is suddenly lowered, the bass will quit feeding for a few days. However, if the drop in water is very slow, it often will trigger a feeding spree. Rising waters also effects them. If the rise is sudden, such as just after a heavy storm, they quit feeding. But if the rise is gradual, the fishing is normally good, especially in the new areas created by the rising waters.

In many respects, bass resemble the cat family as a predator. Have you ever seen a movie of a lion as she creeps through the tall grass trying to get within striking range of her prey? She will move agonizing slow as she begins her stalk, carefully but slowly advancing paw by paw until she is within charging range of her quarry.

Bass often follow a similar procedure. As a lure hits the water, they will frequently ease behind a log or clump of weeds. As it approaches, they will make a slow move toward the lure but then pause briefly. As the lure reaches its closest point, the bass strikes savagely.

The fisherman's knowledge of how a bass attacks his prey can be most helpful. Remember, they like to lie in wait for their quarry. The things that trigger a strike are (1) closeness of the prey, (2) sudden pauses, (3) sudden flight. If you will make your lure do these three things, you can expect plenty of action.

In addition to stalking their prey, bass will often go into a frenzy and apparently kill for the sheet pleasure of it. They have been observed tearing into a school of shad, slashing viciously into the school time after time, leaving crippled and dead shad scattered about.

You should try to remember these various traits of how the bass feeds for it can be most helpful as you try to outwit this famous fighter. We will make additional references to this in later chapters as we discuss different techniques for enticing bass to strike.

CHAPTER 5
SPRING

Spring is the ideal time for taking big bass. Actually, it is the temperature of the water that counts rather than the season. As the water temperature moves from the 50's into the 60's, the bass move into the shallows to spawn. In the deep south, this can occur as early as January. Further north, it may be as late as May. One very dependable sign is when the redbud and dogwood trees are in full bloom. This almost always coincides with the ideal water temperature for spawning. Just remember that your best bet during this period is in shallow water, usually three to six feet deep.

There are many bass fishermen who will not fish during the spawning season. They feel it is wrong to catch fish during this period while they are so vulnerable.

Others feel it is O.K. to try for a trophy bass during this period as long as they release all the smaller ones. It's an individual decision that each fisherman will have to decide for himself.

As the water warms into the low 60's and stays there for about five days, the male moves into shallow water anywhere from 1 1/2 to 5 feet deep. He usually starts building a nest while the water is still to cold to spawn. He cleans an area from one foot to three feet in diameter on the lake or river bottom. This is done by fanning the area clean of silt and debris.

After the water has remained at a suitable temperature for 4 or 5 days, the female bass lays her eggs in the small depression which the male has created for the nest. Occasionally, more than one female will lay her eggs in the same nest. As the eggs are deposited by the female, they are quickly fertilized with milt from the male. The eggs are formed into a glutinous mass and sink into the nest where they become glued to the bottom.

The male is the one that guards the eggs to keep them from being eaten by bluegill and other fish or creatures. He fans the eggs almost constantly with his tail to keep silt from covering them.

The eggs usually hatch from 6 to 12 days. If the water temperature drops, it takes longer for the eggs to hatch. If the water warms up, they hatch much sooner.

The quantity of eggs can fluctuate considerably. A small bass might lay no more than 2,000 eggs whereas a large fish might produce 35,000 or more.

After the eggs are hatched, the young fry remain close to

the nest for several days with the male staying close by to protect them. After that, the small fry have to scatter and shift for themselves as the male suddenly develops a taste for his own offsprings and starts to eat them.

CHAPTER 6
SUMMER

After spawning, bass disperse and move into deepwater hideouts usually in heavy cover. This occurs when the water temperatue moves into the 70's or higher.

They like to take over a territory and will usually hangout around a stump, fallen tree, old creek channel, junction of a creek, rocky hole, pier or dock, sheltered bay, rocky or weedy point, shoreline break, mass of tree roots or undercut ledge.

One point to remember is that when you catch a bass from one of these spots, be sure to mark it. Whatever it was about that spot that appealed to your bass, will also appeal to other bass and they will move in once that area is vacated. You can return later to that same spot from time to time with excellent possibilities for additional catches.

Also, it is always a good idea to make notes of your early morning, mid- morning, mid-day, mid-afternoon and late period activities. Often times a pattern develops when some hatch starts a food-chain activity and your notes can become quite valuable for later years.

Bass are highly unpredictable but during the summer months there are a couple of fairly predictable patterns you can usually count on. Most lakes and reservoirs have several shallow places called bars or shoals. This is a shallow part of the lake that is surrounded by deep water. These are the summer homes for bass and you may consider that as reliable information.

Almost all lakes have bars and shoals. Often times they are formed next to river channels where the current washes in debris such as sand and sediment and the deposits form a bar.

These bars and shoals are prime fishing spots during the summer. In winter, bass like to hole up in deep river channels and other areas not exposed to wind and current. But in the summer they prefer exposed areas, preferably the areas around bars and shoals out in the lake that is frequently swept by wind. They like to find an ambush point and wait for baitfish to come near them. You can often find schools of bass around these bars and shoals and the fishing can be fantastic.

The ideal spot is to find a drop off of the bar or shoal. A sharp drop off is a prime spot for bass. One of the best summer lures for bass that congregate around bars and shoals is a plastic worm. They are hard to beat when summer fishing for bass. When you catch a bass, continue to work the area thoroughly for those areas frequently hold large schools and the fishing can be excellent.

In years past, the pattern of a typical summer bass fisherman was to start fishing around 6:00 A.M. and continue to about 10:00 A.M., then stop until around 4:00 or 5:00 that afternoon and start again. In other words, early morning and late evening were considered the best fishing times for bass. And if he was fishing in shallow waters, he was probably correct.

However, with the development of depth finders and other electronic gear, we now know that during summer months, bass spend about 90 percent of their time in deep water.

Common sense would dictate that if a fisherman can find these deep water hang outs of bass, their chances for catching them will improve considerably. Deep water fishing is not much different than shallow water fishing. You just fish deeper.

It is a good idea to get a contour map of your lake. To the deepwater bass specialist, these contour lines will show where the bass are most likely to be located.

A good time to start your deepwater fishing is in early spring when the water temperatures reach the 50 to 55 degree mark. Find the deepwater point that is adjacent to a shallow water cove. The bass will very shortly be heading into those coves as the water gets warmer and the spawning urge grows stronger.

17

However, prior to spawning, the bass will stay on those points in deep water, moving occasionally for brief periods into shallow water to feed. So if you do any early spring fishing, going for the deepwater bass is your best bet.

During spawning season, you won't have much luck with deepwater fishing. Since all bass do not spawn at the same time, you can still take an occasional deepwater bass. But during spawning, shallow water fishing is by far your best bet for top action.

When deepwater fishing, it is a good idea to use as light a line as possible without risking the loss of the fish. When the water is very clear, a 4-pound test line is recommended. The reason is due to water clarity. Many people are not aware of it, but most of the time deep water is much clearer than surface water. Most bass fishermen prefer a clear blue fluorescent line that is classified as abrasion resistant.

Effective lures for deepwater bass include plastic worms, jigs and spinnerbaits. Move them slowly across the bottom until you've covered the entire area. If these don't draw any strikes, try a deep diving crankbait. Be sure to get the lure down deep where the fish are at.

When using crankbaits, use a light line and a long rod for making very long casts. You can make the lure go deeper by kneeling in the boat and by submerging the rod into the water all the way to within a few inches of the reel. This will permit the lure to run at much greater depths than normal After the spawning season ends and shallow water fishing becomes less productive, move back into the same deepwater areas that were producing in the early spring using the same methods that produced before the spawning season. During this period of early summer, bass can usually be found in water of the 12 to 20 foot range.

As mid-summer approaches and the water heats up to 75 degrees and more, shallow water bass almost disappear. But this is the very period of the year when the deepwater fisherman can have a ball.

During these very hot months, bass move into deeper water, from 15 to 30 feet, depending on the depth of the lake. Search for large underwater structures such as a large boulder or a downed tree. Structures such as these will often harbor from six to two dozen bass. Try a variety of lures in different colors until you find the right combination that start taking fish.

Remember that although bass prefer the comfort and safety of deepwater areas, they still must feed and this often means coming into shallow water where baitfish and other aquatic life are found. So even in hot weather, you can occasionally take a bass in shallow water.

CHAPTER 7
FALL

Fall fishing is a very excellent time to take bass. Fish have a built in mechanism that tells them that winter will soon arrive and they need to store up fat to help them through the frigid months. Almost all fresh water fish feed heavily during the fall months.

The best time for fall fishing are the early morning and late evening hours. The reason is that during those very early and very late hours, the light is diminished to the point that it encourages the smallest life of the aquatic food chain to move about in search of food. This in turns draws out the frogs, crayfish and minnows that feed on these tiny forms of life. And it is the movement of the larger creatures that entice the bass out of their hideouts.

When fishing those early autumn morning hours, your best chance is in the shallows. Later in the morning, as the sun gets higher, the bass move to deeper water. Then late each evening, they move back into the shallows. Adjust your fishing hours according. If you are still fishing the shallows at mid-day after the bass have moved into deeper water, you obviously aren't going to take any. This is probably the most important lesson you can learn about bass fishing. To be successful, you must fish where the bass are at. Acquainting yourself with their feeding habits and how they change during the four seasons can be of enormous value to you.

CHAPTER 8
WINTER

As winter approaches, the top surface water starts to cool and we experience what is called the fall turnover. The cold surface waters sink to the bottom and the lighter, warmer waters that was on the bottom rise to the surface.

As the waters cool, bass desert the shallow shoreline waters and head for the deep. Although winter is probably the least productive time for bass fishing, they can still be taken during those cold months. Look for deep holes where swift streams enter the lake, deep reefs or shoals where the water is 50 or more feet deep, or steep cliffs that slope down to deep water.

Always try to find the warmer waters such as warm springs or inflowing streams. An excellent spot for winter bass is below a dam. The waters coming out of a deep reservoir are much warmer than surface waters and bass will swim upstream to congregate in these warmer tailwaters of the dam.

One point about winter fishing is that you must be very alert for the slightest tap of your lure. Coldwater bass inhale their meals very gently. Set the hook at the slightest hesitation of your lure.

Bright warm spells in the middle of winter can often start bass to feed. This is especially true in southern states. They will usually be schooling along deep, submerged creek channels. The jigging - spoon technique is one of the best ways to take winter bass under these conditions.

CHAPTER 9
DEPTHFINDERS

There is now a wide variety of depthfinders on the market and for the serious bass fisherman, they are almost a must. They cannot, in themselves, help you catch bass, but they can pinpoint the most productive bass waters when used correctly. That is the primary use of depthfinders, to help you find the best potential bass structures such as dropoffs,channel ledges or bottom objects.

Some of the more expensive models can actually show the presence of fish and with some experience, you can even identify which fish it is showing. You simply learn to relate the fish to structure at a given time of the year. For example, striped bass or hybrids would be out in open water, crappie mostly stay in schools and stay suspended over channels, catfish would be close to the bottom and bass would usually be around stumps, dropoffs, grassbeds or rocks.

There are basically three types of depthfinders: flasher types, chart recorder types and liquid - crystal - display types. Your local tackle shop should be able to assist you in explaining how the different types work.

CHAPTER 10
TEMPERATURE GAUGES

A temperature gauge is one of the most important tools a serious bass fisherman can possess. They are most important in the spring and fall but can also be quite helpful year round.

During spring and fall, bass movements to and from shallow water relate mostly to water temperatures. And frequently, a change of only a few degrees will determine whether bass are active or lethargic.

Where different creeks enter the same lake, you will often find a difference of as much as 10 degrees on the same day. Usually the bass are most active in the warmer water. In the spring and fall, a cold front can often drop water temperatures from five to seven degrees overnight which will cause the fish to move to deeper waters.

On hot summer days, a temperature gauge can help you find cool water springs which usually have fish close by. Also, during hot summer, fish will locate in holes of 20 to 25 feet deep. You may have heavy rains for a few days that could cool the waters by as much as 10 degrees in which case the bass may move up to the banks in much shallower water. A temperature gauge can pinpoint these changes.

There are several different styles of temperature gauges. The most common used by bass fishermen are surface - reading units mounted somewhere on their boat which give a temperature reading by simply flipping a toggle switch. Other models have a probe which you lower to a specific depth to obtain a deeper reading.

Water temperature has a definite effect on the actions of bass. The largemouth prefers a temperature range of between 65 degrees and 75 degrees F., whereas the smallmouth likes it slightly cooler, between 60 degrees to 70 degrees F. However, although this is the preferred temperature, largemouths are often taken through the ice from a water temperature of between 34 degrees to 39 degrees F.

In late fall and winter, as waters become colder, the metabolism of bass starts to slow down. They become very sluggish, eat less food, require less oxygen and they don't have much energy to chase a lure. However, if you can find an area where the water is slightly warmer than the surrounding water, such as around a spring, you can almost always find a concentration of bass in that area. An excellent place for winter fishing is just below the discharge area of an electric generating plant. The steam from these plants is first cooled in huge cooling towers, then released into nearby waters, creating a haven for fish in the cold months of winter.

At the other extreme, when water temperature rise above 80 degrees, bass become quite uncomfortable for they require more oxygen. This is when you can find them along windy shorelines as they seek additional oxygen. They will also gather where a spring enters a lake or among aquatic plants that produce oxygen.

From the fisherman's consideration, water temperatures are most important. We know that bass are most active in the 60 to 75 degree range. If the water temperature is around 80 degrees at the surface but about 65 at the bottom, you obviously will want to fish the bottom. A temperature gauge can be most helpful in determining the level at which bass are most likely to be at a given moment.

The temperature at which the largemouth is most comfortable is around 70 degrees. Since water temperatures will fluctuate from one level of the water to another, you will often see the bass move either to a higher or lower level seeking his preferred comfort level.

They will often try to avoid the direct rays of the sun and will seek a shadow of a boat dock, stump, log, lily pad or anything that cast a shadow. Sometimes he will go deeper to avoid the strength of the sun's rays.

These are important things to remember as you try to entice a bass to take your lure. He may be at one level part of the day to find the temperature at which he is most comfortable and at another level later in the day to avoid the sun's rays.

It is very difficult to judge which effects bass the most, light or temperature. They seem to bite better on dull days rather than bright days but this is no set rule. Certainly, there has been many a bass caught on bright days.

A great deal has been written about the thermocline that exists in many lakes. This is referred to as a layer of water that lies between the surface and the bottom.

The temperature range in the thermocline can vary from 45 to 70 degrees. During hot summer months, about 80 percent of all bass will be found in this thermocline layer simply because it has the most comfortable water temperature.

The thickness of the thermocline layer can vary from two feet up to 15 feet. It normally starts at depths of 15 to 25 feet. Obviously, if this is the favorite area of bass during hot summer months, it would be to the interest of the fisherman to find this area and concentrate on putting his lures to that depth. When good structure bottom, such as drop off points or creek channels, are found within the thermocline layer, you have located the supreme area for finding bass.

One way of locating the thermocline layer is to lower a temperature gauge into the water until you find the temperature is dropping one-half degree per foot of depth. You are then in the thermocline layer.

No bass will be found below the lowest level of the thermocline. All bass will be found either in or above the thermocline.

One excellent lure for fishing the thermocline is a jigging spoon. Jig the spoon over deep drops or points, occasionally allowing the spoon to fall all the way to the bottom. Keep a close eye on your lure because you may not feel the strike. Bass almost always take a spoon on the fall.

CHAPTER 11
COLOR METERS

Many test have been conducted which verify that bass can distinguish between colors, even between various shades of a single color. Because of their physical makeup, a bass eye receives five times more light than the human eye which allows them to distinguish shapes, sizes and color patterns under varying water and light conditions which the human eye could not do.

Their eyes also contain a black pigment that shades the photo-sensitive cells of the retina. This pigment is not present in human eyes but is necessary in bass because they have no eyelids. Because of this pigment, they can also see well on bright days with no discomfort.

I won't go into much details on colors but one interesting discovery was that in clear water at nighttime, bass showed a preference for black.With this information, you would be well advised to fish your clear lakes at night with black spinnerbaits or black topwater plugs.

Extensive experiments indicate that during daytime bass can see red and violet best with green being next in line.Both blue and yellow are less distinct than other colors and they seem to have difficulty in distinguishing between yellow and gray.

From the fisherman's standpoint this should be of no great importance. Bass have been taken on virtually every shade and color available.

The important thing to remember is that a particular color that worked wonders today may not draw a strike tomorrow. The solution is to experiment. Your main concern should be to find out what colors are they hitting today.

Fortunately, there is now a tool that can assist you in determining the most favorable color for any given moment.

As of this writing, there is one unit available that can help bass fishermen tell which color lures bass can see best under certain conditions. It is called a Color - C - Lector and was developed by Dr. Loren Hill of the University of Oklahoma.

It has been known for many years that bass are not color blind but Dr. Hill's studies concluded that bass can distinguish between 26 different colors or shades. All of these colors are shown on his Color - C - Lector.

The Color - C - Lector works very similar to a camera's light meter which tells you which exposure to choose. To get your reading, lower a simple light-meter probe into the water to the particular depth you plan to fish. The probe will measure the light intensity and convert it to electrical energy which will push an indicator needle across the color band telling you which color the fish see best at that particular time.

Bill Dance, who is one of the better known professional bass fishermen, was one of the first to use the Color - C -Lector. In trying to determine the value of the Color - C -Lector, he would take a color reading and then choose a lure of a completely different color. Frequently, he would not draw a single strike while using the wrong color even though he knew bass were in the area. He would then switch to the color indicated and would continue fishing the very same waters and would start catching bass. This rather convincingly proved that if you are using the preferred colored lure at the proper time, you will greatly improve your chances.

What the Color - C - Lector tells you is which color shade the bass see best at a certain depth, but it isn't the only color they will hit. You can still draw strikes by selecting colored lures on either side of the primary color. The further away you move from the primary color, the less likely you will be of getting bass that particular day.

Using the proper color lure does not mean you will automatically start catching bass. You still must be in water where the bass are at and you must present your lure correctly. However, most fishermen that have used the Color - C - Lector reported outstanding results.

The Color - C - Lector is powered by a standard 9 - volt radio battery and is small enough to fit in a large tackle box. You can buy one at most leading fishing tackle stores.

CHAPTER 12
pH METERS

All water has a pH which is measured on a scale of 0 to 14. The number 7 is neutral. The most desirable number for bass is 7.5 to 7.9, however they can and often live well outside this range.

The way to use a pH meter is to select the area of a lake you wish to fish. Start taking pH readings at one - foot intervals all the way to the bottom, making notations at each reading. Somewhere between the surface and the bottom will be a distinct break in the pH sequence, possibly only two-tenths of a point. That is the depth where the fish are most likely to be.

Once you have found this preferred depth, move around the area to find cover at this particular depth or look for a deeper channel where you may find bass suspended at that depth.

It is believed that pH is more important in shallow lakes with heavy vegetation. The reason being that photosynthesis can change pH levels throughout the day. It is known that pH determines how well fish can utilize oxygen present in the water which effects the fish's behavior. Water that is too acidic, which has a low pH reading, or too alkaline, which has a high pH, will cause bass to quickly move to another location.

Most fishing tackle stores carry pH meters. They can be mounted permanently on the side of your boat or carried portable.

Learning how to effectively use a pH meter (also temperature gauges, color meters and depthfinders) can be a tricky business. One of the best ways is to go fishing with someone who already knows how to use them and learn by observation. Once you learn the basics and how to utilize the information, you will find these electronic gadgets can greatly improve your ability to locate productive bass waters.

CHAPTER 13
SHALLOW WATER FISHING

There are two times of the year when shallow water fishing for bass can be very effective...in the spring and fall. During the cold months of winter and the hot days of summer; bass, as do most fish, go deep. But in the spring and fall, bass move into the shallows chasing schools of baitfish.

The most effective time for shallow water fishing is when the shoreline has been undisturbed for sometime, such as at nighttime or early of a morning before there are many boats on the water.

As for finding the best shallow water fishing areas, it seems to come with practice and experience. Most bass anglers know what they are looking for. There are certain shoreline contours or surface cover areas that appeal to them. Experience dictates that certain places will hold bass from time to time.

One shallow water technique is to try a topwater minnow - imitation crankbait. Toss it up close to a log, let it rest until the water ringlets disappear then barely twitch it. Don't be caught napping because that little twitch can result in an explosive strike.

CHAPTER 14
DEEPWATER FISHING

No question about it, deepwater fishing requires time, study and practice to develop the necessary skills. And although deepwater bass don't hit as aggressive as shallow water fish, the rewards can still be great because there are a lot more of them in the deep than in the shallows.

And the deepwater specialist has one other advantage over the shallow water practitioner. Bass can also be taken in the winter but only in those deepwater areas. As the water gets cooler, they simply move a little deeper trying to find the most comfortable layer.

Another advantage that deepwater fishing has over shallow water specialists (and this is becoming more important with each passing year), is the effects the boating enthusiasts has on fishing. Each year it seems, more and more people are buying high power boats for water skiing or just to race up and down the lake. They are sometimes referred to by the dedicated fishermen as "water jockeys", "water cowboys" and a few other choice words which wouldn't look too good in print.

When the "water cowboys" are in their boats, shallow water bass fishing drops next to nothing. But the deep water bass will continue to hit. This is a real plus because the boating people have ruined many a fishing trip for the shallow water fisherman but your day can be saved if you deepwater fish for bass.

One thing is for certain. Don't overlook the advantages of deepwater fishing. Your bass fishing just may get a lot better because of it.

CHAPTER 15
SUSPENDED BASS

One of the most difficult fishing challenges is to take bass while they are suspended in deep water. Usually when bass are suspended in deep water, they are not feeding so it requires some imagination to entice them to strike.

One of the more effective techniques to try on suspended bass is to use a jigging spoon. Use a depthfinder or graph recorder to find deepwater areas near good fishing banks. If you find a school of large fish, you most likely have found a school of suspended bass.

Drop a marker over the suspended fish and position your boat directly over them. After finding how deeply the fish are suspended, lower a jigging spoon to that approximate level. Jerk it up about two or three feet, then let it flutter back down through the school. Continue to do this always being alert to set the hook. If the fish takes the lure, it is usually done so while the spoon is falling, most often in the form of a light bump.

CHAPTER 16
NIGHT FISHING

As a fisherman, you may be puzzled as to how a bass can hit a dark lure on a dark night. You can probably visualize the vibration or gurgling noise of the lure and reason that the bass strikes at sound. But what about a dark, plastic worm that makes no such noise. They, too, can take bass at night.

The answer revolves around the lateral line on a bass. This lateral line runs from behind the gills all the way to the tail on both sides of the fish. It is as accurate as radar in locating an object.

Anything that moves through the water has to displace some water even though it may be quite small. It is this minute displacement of water that is picked up by the lateral line and the bass can strike the source of that sound just as deadly as if he were in broad daylight. The lateral line works only within a few feet of the bass. It does not pick up long distance sounds. But if you can put a dark worm on a dark night within a few feet of a bass, he can hit it with deadly accuracy.

However, bass do have ears inside their head, which is in addition to the lateral line. Those ears can pick up sounds a long distance away. The light gurgling of a lure on top of the water can draw their attention. This can be both good and bad. The good part is that we know they can hear out lures. The bad part is that any loud disturbance, such as a tackle box scraping the bottom of a boat or squeaky oarlocks, can send a bass scurrying for cover. Remember, whether night fishing or day fishing, keep the noise to an absolute minimum and you've taken a first step toward increasing your catches.

CHAPTER 17
SLOW FISHING TECHNIQUE

Sometimes when fishing fast isn't drawing any strikes, try fishing slow. When bass are holed up and not very aggressive, you need to drop a slow moving lure almost in front of them to make them hit. One of the best ways to do this is by "flipping".

This technique requires you to move right in close to heavy cover and work a jig or a porkrind attached to a jig. Lower the bait slowly and work it up and down the root wads of stumps, thick treetops, under boat docks or next to large logs. Always be as quite as possible when approaching such spots and when you drop the bait into the water. Work such areas carefully and set the hook forcefully when you feel and unusual bump or tug on your line.

Another slow fishing technique is to cast small plastic worms along deep banks. Keep your boat out in the deep zone and cast perpendicular to the bank. Allow your lure to sink to the bottom. Then gently lift your bait and glide it a short distance toward the deeper water. Then allow it to again sink to the bottom. Continue to do this lift and drop technique all the way back to your boat. Do not make quick jerky movements with your worm. When bass are not hitting fast moving lures, they will often take a properly presented slow moving bait.

CHAPTER 18
FOUL WEATHER TECHNIQUE

During rainstorms, strong winds or other foul weather, bass often move into the shallows to feed. One of the best lures you can use under these conditions is a spinnerbait.

When foul weather bass are in the shallows, try a single - bladed spinnerbait by running it just under the surface leaving a rippling trail behind. Occasionally, speed up your retrieve so the blade breaks the surface. This will imitate a panic - stricken minnow fleeing from a predator and will sometimes incite a bass to strike.

Try adding trailers to your spinnerbait such as a curlytail grub or pork rind. You may wish to spray these with a fish - attractant formula which will leave scent trails in the water.

Try working spinnerbaits slowly through cover. Select one with a long upper arm and a weedguard over the hook. If you don't have a weedless spinnerbait, place a rubber band behind the barb and by stretching it forward over the lure's eye, you can make it weedless. When a fish strikes, it dislodges the rubber band leaving the hook bare and ready to penetrate the fish tissue.

Try changing colors of your spinnerbait blades. I've seen them with a copper finish, gold and silver plated or painted red and white and other assorted colors including some beautiful fluorescent combinations. You want a blade that throws off a flash and provides a great visual attraction to the fish.

CHAPTER 19
FLOATING VEGETATION

Floating vegetation such as water hyacinths, duckweed, water lettuce and water fern provide excellent cover for bass. It is often difficult to fish through these plant masses but bass love the stuff and you can frequently nail some real biggies from those areas.

Most lakes will have a cove or two that is covered with duckweed or other floating plants. They grow in most of our states and when you find an area of a lake that contains this floating vegetation, you may have hit the jackpot for bass fishing spots. A lure dropped through that thick cover is something a bass finds hard to resist.

The idea fishing method is to fish near the top of the water. The reason being that bass lie in the waters and are use to seeing things on the surface such as frogs trying to walk over the duckweed. So you need to have a lure with top water action that can be seen from below.

Cast your lures and let them fall upon the green carpet. To the bass, this will sound just like a frog or some other creature and he is almost certain to investigate to see what made the sound.

Twitch the lure slowly and "walk" it over the plants and weeds as you retrieve it. Try to hit small openings in the heavy weedscape. Allow the lure to rest a few seconds before starting your retrieve. There will be plenty of times your lure won't make it back to the boat as an exploding bass hits it.

Your selection of a lure is very important. Weedless, flexible rubber plugs are an ideal choice or any lure that you can keep close to the surface. You don't want a lure that is too light that it just remains on top of the vegetation. Bass will normally not pop through the surface to hit an unseen object. You want a lure that will penetrate the vegetation. One excellent retrieve is to keep the lure just below the surface but have the nose of the lure ripple the surface every foot or two. This is called the "dropping lure" pattern and can be very effective in drawing vicious strikes.

Many anglers make the mistake of either avoiding floating vegetation or else casting only around its edge. You will get few bass this way. The bass are back in under the vegetation and you must get your lure back into that area for the fast action. It is best to use heavy line in the 20 to 30 pound range as weed abrasion will take its toll on lighter monofilament.

CHAPTER 20
BRIDGE FISHING

Almost every lake has a hot spot and one of the most productive hot spots is fishing around bridges. Look on your state map at the various man made lakes. You will notice that almost all have backwaters that extended over county and state roads that are now passable only because bridges were built over the fingers of the lakes.

Some of these bridges cover water that is quite shallow and therefore not very productive. But many of them are over old creek channels or areas where the water is several feet deep and they are fantastic producers of bass during certain parts of the year.

There are various reasons for this. For one thing, the bridge provides a shade during hot summer months. Also, the pilings or structures that support the bridge are excellent hiding places to attack an unsuspecting victim swimming by. And in addition to this, shad and other minnows congregate at the bridges by the thousands which give the bass another very good reason to also be there.

In spring, during spawning season, the bridge fishing will

be very poor. You may take a few small bass too young to spawn but all of the larger bass will be off in the shallows reproducing.

However, as soon as spawning season is over, they will move to the bridges in large numbers. This is an excellent time to fish the bridges. For those few weeks after spawning and until hot weather sets in, the fishing around bridges can be fast and furious.

After hot weather arrives, many of the bass will move into deeper water and the fishing drops off although you can still take a few especially if the water under the bridge is over 15 feet deep.

When fall arrives, the fishing around the bridges again becomes highly productive. In winter,it drops back to about the same as the hot weather months. You can still take a few in winter but only around bridges that span deep channels.

So remember, if you are looking for a bass hot spot, try fishing around bridges in early spring before spawning, in late spring after spawning and in all of the autumn months.

CHAPTER 21
BUMPING THE STUMP TECHNIQUE

A very effective technique for taking bass is to find an area where tree stumps or logs are located in about 15 feet of water. Most all lures will work when using this technique; buzzbaits, jigs, plugs, spinnerbaits, plastic worms, crankbaits, etc.

Cast your lure several feet beyond the stump or log. Then with a slow, steady retrieve, guide the lure with your rod tip toward the stump, allowing it to bump into the object. On diving lures, you will occasionally experience a snag but you will draw many a strike because bass hide out around logs and the root system of those old tree stumps and it is hard for them to resist hitting when you put the lure so close to home.

CHAPTER 22
FISHING RIPRAP BANKS

No doubt you have seen in most man - made lakes large banks of rocks. They will often be lining causeways, earthen dams, marina jetties, lakefront lawns and upstream ends of islands. They were put there to stop or prevent erosion by water currents and waves. These are called riprap rocks or riprap banks and quite often they can provide excellent bass fishing.

There are several reasons why riprap is so attractive to bass. First, bass like to take cover around rocks. It is one of their favorite hangouts. Second, a riprap bank is normally loaded with various type of baitfish such as shad and bluegill which feed on the algae and other life clinging to the rocks. The rocky crevices also hold large quantities of crayfish.

Third, a point jutting out into a bay or a roadway crossing a lake would already be a natural hangout for fish. Add rocks which will automatically increase the food supply and you almost certainly have increased the bass supply right along with it.

However, not all riprap will produce the desired results. Small, tightly fitted rocks normally don't produce. Big, rough cut rocks will attract more bass than the smaller rocks. Also, the location is important. Riprap rising out of shallow water will produce few bass. You will find far more bass when the riprap descends into deep water. Although you can take bass in the plain, featureless areas, you can do much better if you can find and abnormality in the riprap pattern such as an indentation, washed up logs or a rockslide. These irregular spots will normally hold larger concentrations of bass.

As winter comes to an end, bass start feeding heavily to build up energy reserves for the coming spawn. They head for the warmest water they can find and if you have a riprap bank facing the sun, you have an ideal situation. The rocks catch the sun's rays and in turn warms up the water. Fishing such located riprap banks can often be your best early season fishing. Worms and jig and porkrind combinations are favorite baits while the water is still cold. Whichever bait you use for early spring riprap fishing, they must be fished extremely slow to be effective.

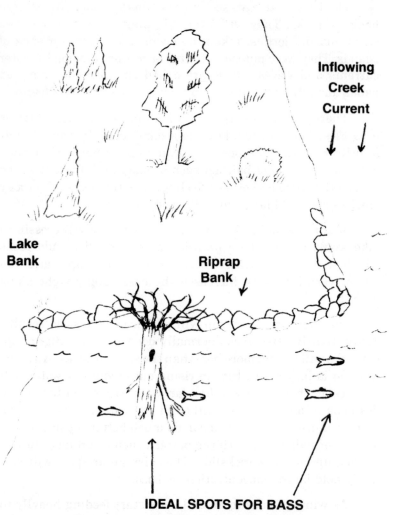

Inflowing Creek Current

Lake Bank

Riprap Bank

IDEAL SPOTS FOR BASS

Around broken areas of a riprap bank such as a fallen tree and on the downstream side of jetty points where bass congregate waiting for baitfish to swim by.

As the water warms in late spring and early summer, a wide variety of lures will work on the properly situated riprap bank. One point to remember, if the water is rather clear, riprap fishing usually diminishes since the bass can see your boat and will move into deeper water. Another important consideration is to try and locate a point with a riprap bank that extends into the current of an incoming stream. Fish on the down - current side of the point casting your lure to the edge of the point and retrieving it with the current. Bass love to hang out along the riprap waiting for schools of baitfish to migrate into the main channel and for the current to sweep them past. Concentrate at points where the current swirls around the rocks. As baitfish are swept into view, the bass nail them. Obviously, if you can put your lures into these hop spots, you can expect some fast action.

CHAPTER 23
FISHING SPOONS

Here's the way spoons supposedly originated. As the story goes, a gentleman was fishing and stopped long enough to grab a snack. As he reached into his lunch box, he accidentally knocked a teaspoon into the water. He watched helplessly as the spoon wobbled toward the lake bottom. Suddenly the long dark shape of a northern pike darted from a nearby weed bed to attack the spoon.

No dummy, this fellow, for he quickly realized he might be on to something. He later sniped off the handles of several teaspoons, drilled holes in both ends, one for attaching a hook and the other his line. Thus was born the fishing spoon.

As to whether this story is true or not, no one knows. But one thing we do know is that spoons in various shapes, sizes and colors are excellent lures for taking bass.

Spoons do not wiggle and vibrate wildly as spinnerbaits and crankbaits do. Instead, they wobble casually through the water with a natural movement that draw strikes.

When bass are deep, jigging a spoon is quite effective. Other methods for working a spoon in deep water is to hop the spoon back to your boat in a series of rhythmic skips. You can also allow it to lie on the lake bottom for several seconds before reeling it up a few feet and them allowing it to drop back to the bottom. You should also try jerking upon the rod tip and then let the spoon flutter down. You should try this several times in succession.

When fishing spoons, be alert for anything. Set the hook the moment you feel or sense something unusual. Often times, a slight line twitch will be the only clue that a bass has taken the lure.

When spoon fishing shallow water, a good technique is to spot a structure in the water such as a large stump. Cast your spoon well beyond the stump, then reel in quickly until the spoon is near the stump. Now stop reeling and allow the spoon to flutter enticingly toward the bottom. You can draw plenty of strikes as your spoon flutters downward.

Spoons can also be made effective by adding a porkrind strip, twister - tail grub or a rubber vinyl skirt. Spoons can also draw some hard strikes from big bass when trolling. Be sure to troll at different depths. Make a lot of slow turns. As you make these sharp, slow turns, your spoon will start to flutter downward frequently drawing a vicious strike.

CHAPTER 24
BUZZBAITS

Buzzing for bass can be one of your most productive techniques for taking largemouths from heavy cover such as moss, weeds, brush and downed trees.

When fishing these areas that are thick with trees and brush, the problem is getting your lure into the hiding holes and then getting the bass out. Buzzbaits provide the answer for bass fishing these obstacle - loaded lakes.

If you've never seen a buzzbait in action, you will probably wonder how on earth could you catch a bass on it. You would think it would scare the bass away with all the gurgling, buzzing, sputtering and plopping noises it makes. But nothing could be further from the truth. The noise apparently makes the bass mad and they will hit the lures repeatedly.

When bass hit a buzzbait, you know it. There is no gentle tapping as you may experience on some other baits. They make vicious strikes at the buzzbait and usually hook themselves without any assistance from the fisherman. They will often follow these fast moving lures for many feet creating a small wake in the water.

Buzzbaits are primarily top water lures and are most effective when bass would be feeding near the surface. They are relatively weedless lures and can be tossed right into the trees and brush of shallow waters. Spring and fall are the two best times to fish the buzzbait lures as this is when bass are usually in the shallows and close to the surface. However, on hot summer days, you can occasionally pull a largemouth from under the shade of a overhanging tree with a fast moving buzzbait.

There are many styles of buzzbaits to choose from as many different companies manufacture them. I'll list just a few which you should be able to obtain at your local tackle shop: Pomme Special, Jumping Jack, Hawg Buzz, Mister Twister Lunker Buzz, Whopper Buzz and Blakemore Double Choice Buzzer. All of these are excellent choices.

The best method for fishing buzzbaits is to hold your rod tip high and start the retrieve before the lure hits the water. You want the lure to be starting back toward you as soon as it hits the water. Try to keep the lure on the surface with it bubbling and buzzing as you retrieve it.

If the lure sinks below the surface you need to crank extra fast to get the lure back on top. The ideal speed for retrieving buzzbaits is to move it as slow as possible while keeping it on top of the water. Too fast of a retrieve will make too much noise while too slow of a retrieve will allow the lure to sink below the surface which prevents it from working properly.

CHAPTER 25
PLASTIC WORM

The plastic worm was first developed in the early 1950's. There are many bass pros that now rank it as the number one lure for its bass - catching ability.

When the plastic worm was first developed, most fishermen rigged it with two or three weedless hooks stretched along the body of the worm. The thinking back then was that a bass struck the worm in different areas. The object was to have as many hooks as possible so that no matter where the bass hit the worm, he could be hooked.

Somewhat later, it became apparent that a bass almost always hits the worm in the same spot, either at the head or close behind it. Once this was learned, anglers started burying a plain hook in the front part of the body of the worm. The favorite was a Sproat hook because it had a straight shank with a small eye which didn't tear the plastic as the worm slid over the eye of the hook.

It is very important that your worm be rigged properly. The hook should be inserted all the way through the head, then turned and the barb of the hook should be buried in the body of the worm making it a weedless lure. After inserting the hook, hold your line and let the worm dangle. If it hangs straight, you have it rigged properly. If there is a bow in the worm, it means you have set the barb too far back and this will cause the worm to spin and twist your line giving it an unnatural action which will greatly reduce its effectiveness.

In addition to how it is rigged, choice of color is very important. Although bass have been caught on virtually every color in existence, the five colors that are most popular among the majority of bass fishermen are purple, black, red, avocado and blue but not necessarily in that order. Normally, the darker colors do better on cloudy days and at night. The lighter colors seem to catch more fish on bright days when the water is fairly clear.

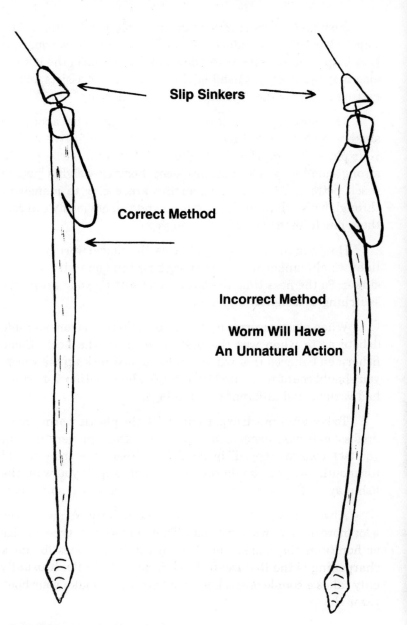

Slip Sinkers

Correct Method

Incorrect Method

**Worm Will Have
An Unnatural Action**

RIGGING A PLASTIC WORM
Hold your line and let the worm dangle. If it hangs straight, you
have it rigged correctly. If the worm is bowed, you have set the
hook too far back resulting in an unnatural appearance.

Perhaps even more important than colors is the slip sinker. Slip sinkers give you added weight for casting the worm, plus they help in getting the worm down to the bottom of the lake. It also helps protect the head of the worm and it assists you in getting a feel for the type bottom you are fishing.

The most important thing you should remember about slip sinkers is that the lighter they are, the more effective will be your plastic worm. Heavier sinkers also serve a purpose. In a strong current, you sometimes need heavier weights just to reach bottom. Also heavier weights are easier to maneuver through brush than the lighter ones and you obviously can cast them much further than light weights.

However, in the majority of cases, the rigged worm with the light weight sinker will catch more bass than one with a heavy sinker. So the next time the bass aren't hitting your worm, try switching to a lighter slip sinker.

When plastic worms first came out, there was considerable debate as to when was the best time to set the hook. Some fishermen believed that when you felt a bass pick up the worm, you should count to ten and then set the hook. Other fishermen had various and different count delays.

Today, after much experience with the plastic worms, most professional bass fishermen now believe that the very instant you feel a worm "tapped" by a fish, he already has the worm in his mouth and you should set the hook at once. If you wait, the fish may realize that the worm is artificial and will spit it out.

Always be sure your hooks are needle sharp. You will catch a lot more bass with sharp hooks. There are several types of files or hones on the market but one of the better ones for hook sharpening is the Red Devil Wood Scraper #15 File. It usually only takes a couple of strokes with this tool to make your hook razor sharp.

CHAPTER 26
JIGS

A jig is nothing more than a lead head molded on a hook which is finished off by tying on feathers or bucktail. It can be far more effective for bass by adding a strip of pork rind or an artificial tail called an eel. A jig is most effective when the water temperature drops below 60 degrees.

There are basically two ways to fish jigs. One, by using it as a fall bait (that is a bait that fish will hit while it is sinking) or, two, by bottom bouncing. Bass almost always hit jigs while they are falling. For this reason, you don't want the lure resting on the bottom nor do you want to drag it across the bottom. Instead, once the lure hits bottom, lift it up three or four feet and let it fall again. Continue to walk it across the bottom or down cliffs or ledges in this manner being always on the alert for a strike while the bait is falling.

Just as with the slip sinker on the plastic worm, you want to use the lightest jig head possible. You want the head to be heavy enough to take the lure to the bottom but no heavier.

When fishing with a jig, keep your eye on the line, especially as the lure is falling. Most often your strike will be seen as a flick of the line. Set the hook immediately when you see this happen. A difficult situation occurs when the bass takes the jig and starts moving toward you. When this happens, the only way you can detect it is the feel of a weightless sensation with the rod. If this happens, start cranking fast and when the line comes tight, then set the hook.

CHAPTER 27
SPINNER BAITS

Spinner baits have been around for many years but only in recent times have bass fishermen begun to realize the year-round importance of this lure. When bass tournament fishing was in its infancy, over 80 percent of the fish were caught on plastic worms. But with passing time, the spinner baits became more and more popular and it would be difficult today to find a professional bass fisherman that doesn't carry several spinner baits at all times.

One of the big advantages of spinner baits is that they will take bass twelve months of the year. It can be fished a number of ways and you are limited only by your imagination. It can be fished on the bottom, on the surface, just under the surface or as a fall bait. Almost anything you can do with the variety of other baits, you can also do just as effectively with a spinner bait.

There are basically three types of spinner baits. One is the single spin. It has a single blade and is the most popular of the three styles. Second is the tandem spin which has two blades mounted on the same shaft. Third is the twin spin which has two shafts with a blade on each shaft.

Spinner baits can be very effective around such objects as brush piles, fallen trees, stumps, rocks or most any other large objects. Start out by buzzing the bait on the surface past these objects. When the spinner runs on top of the water with the blade breaking the surface, it is referred to as "gurgle buzz". Colorado spinner blades are best for the gurgle buzz but you need to hold your rod tip high and start the retrieve the instant the lure hits water.

If this method doesn't draw any strikes, try buzzing it just under the surface so that it creates a wake in the water. Once again, you need to hold the rod tip high and start cranking as soon as the lure hits water but your retrieve is slower so that the lure works just below the surface. You may wish to combine this method with the gurgle buzz by occasionally having the lure break through the surface water.

A third method is instead of the steady, buzzing retrieve, cast your spinner bait well past the object, then buzz it to the surface. Now, stop cranking and let the lure fall for a couple or three feet, then start cranking again. You can do this several times during the retrieve. Often times, this method will produce when the steady buzzing won't draw a strike.

A fourth method is to let your spinner bait sink to the

bottom and then crawl it along. This is especially effective when you can crawl the lure past large objects that serve as hiding places for bass. Be sure to try the crawl and stop technique as it is often more effective than a steady crawl. When using this crawling method, be especially alert as the lure is falling. Often times, if bass are suspended, they will nail the lure while it is sinking toward the bottom.

CHAPTER 28
VIBRATING BAITS

Vibrating baits were originally patterned after a saltwater baitfish called the piggy perch which is a member of the grunt family. Although first developed as a saltwater lure, it was later tried in freshwater and found to be very effective in taking bass.

It is almost impossible to fish the vibrating baits incorrectly as they have their own built-in action. However, you don't want to use a large snap or swivel as these large items can effect the action of the lure. Also, it is best not to tie the lure directly to the line as this too does not produce the best action. The vibrating lures respond best when attached to a very small snap.

CHAPTER 29
TAIL SPIN LURES

Tail Spin lures, as the name implies, has a spinner blade attached to the tail of the lure. It can be used as a falling lure and is also effective when fished just under the surface. The blade traps air near the surface resulting in an underwater noise that attracts fish. The flashing spinner blade is also a fish attractor.

Another excellent technique with this lure is to let it settle to the bottom. Then sweep your rod tip up and back forcing the lure to jump as much as six feet. When you drop the rod tip, the lure flutters back to the bottom, often drawing a strike. It can also be bounced or hopped across the bottom.

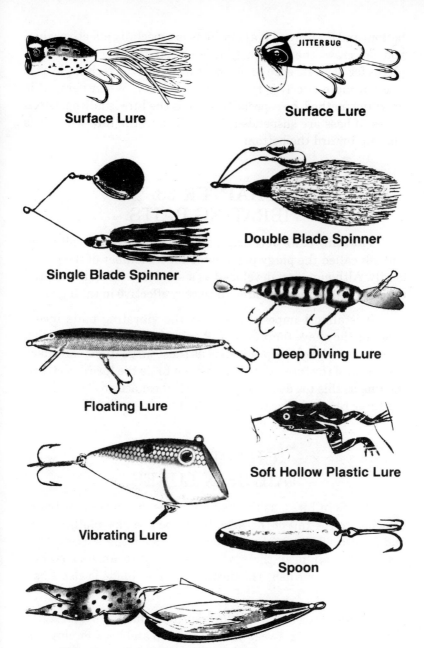

Surface Lure

Surface Lure

Double Blade Spinner

Single Blade Spinner

Deep Diving Lure

Floating Lure

Soft Hollow Plastic Lure

Vibrating Lure

Spoon

Weedless Spoon With Pork Rind

A FEW EXCELLENT BASS LURES

CHAPTER 30
DIVING BAITS

Diving baits are easily identified by the lip in front of the plug. They are often called "crank baits" or "bill baits". The reason they are called diving baits is because the faster you crank the handle of your reel, the deeper they dive.

Most diving baits float on the surface prior to starting the retrieve. They dive only when you start cranking. Stop the retrieve and they will again float back to the surface.

There are various techniques for fishing diving baits. Some fishermen like to crank just as fast as possible making the lure dive deep and swim fast. No question, it is an effective method, for many a fishermen has reported vicious strikes as a bass darts out to take the lure.

Another method is to start a fast retrieve, then stop and allow the lure to start floating toward the surface, then start the fast retrieve again. Continue this crank and pause all the way to your boat. Very often, you will find that a crank and pause method will draw more strikes than a steady retrieve regardless of what lure you are using or what type of fish you are after.

Occasionally, try cranking the bait until it digs in the mud. It will leave a small trail of mud puffs and on certain days, this method will take bass when other efforts are not producing.

Also, try casting a diving bait into the shallows. As you retrieve, guide the lure toward some object such as a tree stump. When the lure is along side the object, stop for a moment to allow the lure to start floating upward. Then start the retrieve again. Your strikes will come just as the lure starts to float upward or just as you resume the retrieve.

CHAPTER 31
CASTING

If you have ever watched a professional bass fisherman, one thing you probably noticed was that he was a very accurate caster. They can place a lure just about anyplace they wished. And they could do it whether they were fishing with fly rod, bait casting or spinning gear.

There is nothing more frustrating than to hang a lure in the brush pile rather than have it fall along side as you intended. If this ever happens, you might as well move to another spot because you have spooked any fish in the area.

You will learn that if you can cast your lure on a precise spot, you will start taking fish on a more consistent basis. Accurate casting is something that can be learned if you are willing to spend the time. It takes practice. I urge you to spend whatever time is necessary until you can drop your lure consistently on a chosen spot.

The best time to do your practicing is between fishing trips. Practice on land. Don't waste your precious fishing time. A few minutes each day practicing in your backyard or a nearby park can work wonders. Pick out a target and try to hit it on every practice cast.

CHAPTER 32
LIVE BAIT

Although many bass fishermen refuse to use anything but lures (and no question about it, many bass are caught on artificial lures), the actual truth is that more bass are caught on live bait than lures.

The reason, perhaps, is simply because the baits are alive. No artificial lure can exactly duplicate the living vibrations of live bait. It is also possible that live bait have an odor that no chemist can duplicate. Artificial lures obviously do not taste alive.

But for whatever reason, live baits will catch more bass than artificial lures. This is especially true when the fishing conditions are toughest. In fact, think back to the first bass you ever caught. If you are like the majority of fishermen, your first bass was probably caught on live bait, perhaps while you bank fishing.

The fact that plastic worms are so successful in taking bass should certainly tell you that a nightcrawler will do the same. One thing that bass don't like is dead bait. They are not scavengers in the sense of catfish and carp. If you fish with worms, keep them alive. When putting them on your hook, make sure that part of the worm is dangling so they can wiggle and look alive. One excellent method is to use a treble hook and put two or three worms on at the same time. It will look like a ball of worms but it will catch bass.

I will list a few other live baits that bass find hard to resist. You will probably have difficulties in finding many of these baits but if you can locate them, you will have a fine chance of bringing home your share of bass. Bass love most all type of minnows, crawfish, frogs, crickets, live shrimp, hellgrammites, catalpa worms, grasshoppers, leeches, salamanders, water dogs, cicadas (17 year locust), softshell crabs, small eels six to eight inches long, golden shiners and many small fish. Small bluegill two to three inches long are very effective in taking bass but be sure to check your state law before using them., Since bluegill are considered to be a sport fish, some states make it illegal to use them as bait.

If you are after big bass, use a minnow at least four inches long. In Florida, bass fishermen often use golden shiners 10 to 12 inches long when they go after the really big trophy bass.

Match your minnow to the size of your hook. Minnows will usually remain active longer if hooked lightly behind the dorsal fin. It is also very effective if hooked through both lips. When fishing large minnows, you may want to use tandem hooks, inserting one through the lips and the other behind the anal fin.

Live minnows make a deadly bass bait when rigged below

The Deadliest Bass Lure of All —
The Live Minnow

And Three Ways To Hook Him

Through the lips for winddrifting or slow trolling in deep water.

Through the back for fishing directly below your boat.

Through the tail allowing the minnow freedom to move under dense cover.

a bobber. However, you should not use sinkers as they will interfere with the action of the minnow. You want your minnow to swim freely and he can do this best when there are no sinkers. A lively minnow near good bass cover such as submerged logs, stumps, or brush is indeed an effective way to take plenty of bucketmouths. If you fail to take a bass within 20 minutes move to another likely spot.

There are three methods for hooking a live minnow.

One is through the lips being careful not to enter the brain area. This method is used when wind drifting or slow trolling in deep water.

Two, hook the minnow through the upper half about midway between head and tail. This method is for vertical fishing when you want your line to go straight down such as bank fishing or fishing directly below your boat. It is usually a good idea to use a bobber when fishing in this manner.

Three, hook the minnow through the tail. This gives the minnow freedom to swim back under dense cover which you can't possibly reach with an artificial lure.

For hot summertime fishing, you will find crayfish, nightcrawlers and salamanders to be excellent baits. Hook the crayfish through the tail, nightcrawlers through the head and salamanders through both lips. Use barrel- sinker rigs which allows you to walk the bait over the bottom.

CHAPTER 33
FARM PONDS

Don't overlook farm ponds as a prime spot for big bass. If you have ever read Sports Afield's Fishing Awards winners, you know that a large number of the largest bass are caught from these small farm ponds.

Here are some of the advantages of the farm pond. First, they are numerous. Farm ponds are scattered across the entire United States. In all probability, within a few miles of where you live are some excellent farm ponds loaded with bass. So this is one of the nice advantages is that you don't have to go far to find one.

Second, a well managed farm pond can produce high yields of bass and other fish. It has been proven that the average farm pond is not fished nearly as often as it should be. Ponds that are not fished very often soon are over populated and all the fish become stunted because of a lack of food. But a pond fished rather frequently keep the population thinned out with the result of larger fish.

One exception to the stunted growth is the bass. When you have bass and bluegill in the same pond, the bass gorge on the small bluegill and grow fat and sassy.

One unfortunate side effect of having bass and bluegill in the same small pond is that sometimes they get out of balance. Bluegill are prolific breeders and occasionally they out multiply the bass so rapidly that bass find it impossible to reproduce.

Although they continue to spawn, they simply can't defend the eggs against hundreds of hungry bluegill.

When this happens, it results in the bass eventually being thinned out to possibly not more than two or three bass in the pond. But what bass they become. These few survivors often reach the 14 to 15 pound range.

Another advantage is that you don't need a lot of expensive gear, not even a boat. Just drive out with a rod and reel and a few lures or live bait and that is all you need to start putting bass on your stringer. Even if it is a large farm pond; a canoe, small johnboat or an inflatable would be quite adequate.

Farm ponds, of course, are on private property and are not available for public fishing. You have to get permission and this can usually be obtained by simply approaching the farmer and asking in a courteous manner. Tell him what day you would like to fish and who will be with you. Occasionally, you will be denied permission but in the majority of cases, you will find the owner will grant permission when properly requested.

CHAPTER 34
POSITIVE ATTITUDES

This may sound silly but most professional bass fishermen will tell you that the most important element of the successful bass fisherman is mental attitude. You must have total confidence in your approach and in the lure you are using. It doesn't matter if you are using a plastic worm or a spinner or if you are fishing the shallows or a deep sloping bank; you must have confidence in what you are doing.

Never allow yourself to get discouraged. If you have a bad day and failed to make a catch, review the techniques you used and the type of places you fished. Try to profit from your experience. Ask yourself if there was some procedure you failed to try.

Remember, the primary reason you love bass fishing is because bass are so very unpredictable. There will be days when you'll catch them almost as fast as you can cast your lure. Other days, you won't be able to get a strike no matter what you try. In fact, if you could outsmart the bass on every cast, you would soon get tired of it. It is the unpredictability of the bass that makes this such a challenging sport.

It is always a good idea at the end of each fishing day to check with other fishermen as to how they did. You should do this whether you were successful or not. This type of information can greatly add to your knowledge of bass fishing.

Were all the fishermen getting skunked for that day? If so, that could indicate there was nothing wrong with your technique. The fish just weren't biting.

Did one fisherman come in with his limit? Find out what type of lure he was using. What depth was he fishing? Make notes. This type of information can be invaluable for later fishing trips.

Knowledge of what you are doing helps to build confidence and a positive attitude and you gain knowledge through experience, asking questions and reading good books and magazine articles on bass fishing. Remember that confidence is crucial to your success so keep pecking away at these things that will build confidence.

CHAPTER 35
MOVING TO ANOTHER LOCATION

One of the first problems facing a new bass fisherman is deciding how long to fish each location. The answer revolves around your confidence. Once you lose confidence in a certain area, you might as well move on, if for no other reason than to regain your confidence. If you lose confidence, you won't have the concentration and you will simply be going through the motions.

Usually, you will want to work an area until you have covered it thoroughly at all depths using a variety of lures and colors. It is also a good idea to try a few variations in the retrieve. Sometimes you can determine with just a few casts that an area is not going to produce. Other times, you may want to spend two hours.

Experience is the key. After you have done a lot of bass fishing, you soon get a feel for where the bass should be. You even develop a knack for the type of lure and the type of retrieve you should use for various situations. Without question, experience will play a great role in determining how long you should fish each spot on a given day.

Many veteran bass fishermen can approach a spot, make a half dozen casts and know immediately if it is worth fishing that area any longer. It is something you too can acquire with experience.

CHAPTER 36
TROPHY BASS

A trophy bass is any bass you would be proud to hang on your wall. It could be a five pound fish for the young fisherman to one of ten pounds or better for the experienced pro. You may wish to note that out of every 6,000 bass fry, only one will survive the perils and hazards of growing up underwater to reach a trophy size of 11 inches. So when you take a 10-pounder or better, you certainly deserve the right to call him a trophy bass.

For trophy bass in the 10 pound range, you need strong gear; heavy duty rods, lines and lures. I would suggest a rod of seven to eight feet with a 40-pound test line. A 10-pound bass has awesome power and can easily snap a lighter line when it is pulled against underwater structures such as logs, tree limbs, stumps and other cover where bass hang out.

However, heavy duty gear is not practical for normal bass fishing. For the average size bass in the 2-pound to 5-pound range, you should use standard rods, reels, line and lures. A rule of thumb is that your line should test about 3 to 1 in relation to the weight of the fish. In other words, for a 2-pound bass, you would want a 6-pound test line. For a 3-pound bass you should have a 10 - pound line. When fishing areas with heavy, snaggy objects move up to the next highest test line.

Using test line in the 6 to 10 pound range should allow you to cast a wide variety of lures from one-quarter ounce and up. One point to remember is that if you are going for the big fellow, make sure the points of your hooks are extra sharp for the simple reason that the jaws of trophy bass are quite hard.

CHAPTER 37
USING A GUIDE

Bass fishing can be rather expensive if you let it, but here is one investment that can pay big dividends.

If you are traveling to a distant lake for a few days of fishing, you can hardly go wrong by hiring a guide for at least the first day. It will cost you from $80 to $150 depending upon how good or how much is the demand for a particular guide. Make inquiries and select one that was well recommended.

You can learn more about that lake in one day from a local guide than you could in several weeks of solo fishing. Get him to show you where are the hot spots for that particular time of the year and what you should look for as you fish by yourself for the balance of your trip. It can often mean the difference between a successful or unsuccessful fishing trip.

CHAPTER 38
BOOKS ON BASS FISHING

If you really have a desire to become a professional bass fisherman, I strongly encourage you to read several good books on bass fishing. I will list a few of the better ones which I highly recommend you read. You can borrow them from your public library. Or, better still, in my opinion, go to your local book store and ask them to order the books for you. Of course, you have to pay for them, but they then become a part of your personal library and will always be available to you for future reference.

Lucas On Bass Fishing by Jason Lucas, 1947, Dodd, Mead & Co., 79 Madison Ave., New York, N.Y. 10016

Bass Angler's Guide by Max Hunn, 1982, Stackpole Books, P.O. Box 1831, Harrisburg, Pa. 17105

Bass Tackle and Tactics by Harold C. Hollis, 1945, A.S. Barnes & Co., 11175 Flintkote Ave., San Diego, CA. 92121

Tactics On Bass by Ray Ovington, 1983, Charles Scribner's Sons, 597 Fifth Ave., New York, N.Y. 10017

Bass : An In-Fisherman Handbook Of Strategies by Bobby Murray, Al Lindner, Chet Meyers, Ron Lindner, and Billy Murray, 1981, Al Lindner's Outdoors, P.O. Box 999, Brainerd, Mn. 56401

Advanced Bass Fishing by John Weiss, 1976, E.P. Dutton, 2 Park Ave., New York, N.Y. 10016

Catch More Bass by Stan Fagerstrom, 1973, The Coxton Printers, Caldwell, Id. 83605

Largemouth Bass by Don Oster, 1983, The Hunting and fishing Library, 5900 Green Oak Dr., Minnetonka, Mn. 55343

How to Fish for Smallmouth by Hank Andrews, 1979, Contemporary Books, 180 N. Michigan Ave., Chicago, Ill. 60601

Practical Black Bass Fishing by Mark Sosin and Bill Dance, Crown Publishers, Inc., New York, 1974

Complete Book of Bass Fishing by Grits Gresham, Outdoor Life, Harper & Row, New York, London, 1966

TECHNIQUES FOR CRAPPIE

CHAPTER 1
THE CRAPPIE AND THE FISHERMAN

Most every fisherman has his favorite fish. For many its the bass, others the trout, pike, musky or perhaps the coho. I've met fishermen who will fish only for carp and others that wouldn't touch anything except a catfish. And then there is the breed of fishermen who feel the bluegill is the only fish that's worth going after. But if you want to meet a loyal, devoted fisherman, just talk to one that's hung up on crappie fishing. Once they get bit by the crappie bug, they seem to concentrate exclusively and wholeheartedly on this one fish.

In the spring of the year when the dogwood and the honeysuckle are starting to bloom, the warming weather soon draws the crappie into the shallow waters to begin their annual spawning activities. To millions of fishermen this is crappie time and you can see them making a mad scramble for their favorite lake, many driving hundreds of miles. It would almost seem that everybody and his uncle had suddenly decided that today would be a good day to go fishing. It is not unusual to see some lakes dotted with boats of every conceivable description and the shoreline literally lined elbow to elbow with crappie fishermen.

For some reason or another, many fishermen seem to believe that crappie can be caught only in the spring of the year. This is simply not true. Crappies can be caught anytime of the year from January through December. You need only to learn something of their habitat, plus a few other tricks, and you can bring home a heavy stringer of crappies most anytime, including after dark. Unlike many other fish that often call it quits when the sun sets, the crappie, with his voracious appetite, keeps right on feeding well into the night.

Without question, the crappie is one of the finest tasting fish in North America. Perhaps that partially accounts for their popularity. They can be found in lakes or streams, in northern or southern waters and in all forty- eight of our local states. If you should ever tie into a school of crappies, don't worry about depleting their number. Crappies are prolific breeders and will multiply by the thousands where conditions are right.

In this book, you will find listed many techniques that have worked for other crappie fishermen. The book was also designed to acquaint you with the seasonal habitat of the crappie. A technique that works beautifully one month, may not work at all two months later because the crappie changes his habitat from season to season. By combining the various techniques along with a knowledge of where the crappie is at during a given season, I an confident you will find that crappie fishing can be a rewarding experience anytime of the year.

CHAPTER 2
SPRING SPAWNING SEASON

Many fishermen insist that spring is the best time for catching crappies. When the water warms up to around 64 to 68 degrees F., the crappies move into shallow water to spawn. This is the time you should be on the water for they can be easily caught all day long.

Normally, crappies spawn in water 2 to 7 feet deep, although occasionally they may go as deep as 8 to 10 feet. It is the male that forms out a nest and then drives one or two females into it. After fertilization, the male guards the nest until the fry can make it on their own. It is during this period that the males will strike anything that comes near the nest. So if you want some surefire crappie action, remember these figures during their spawning season-- a water depth of 2 to 7 feet at temperatures around 64 to 68 degrees.

Of course, you need more information than this. There will be many areas around a lake at this depth and temperature that will contain no crappies and you obviously can't catch crappies if there are no crappies there. Happily, this is a hazard that can be held to a bare minimum for crappies normally follow a distinct pattern in selecting a spawning site.

Crappies have a very definite liking for sheltered bays and coves that contain large brush piles, hollow stumps, weedy areas or any kind of sunken debris. Often they will make their nest in the end of a hollow log or next to large brush piles. Weedy areas with open pockets are especially good. They will frequently spawn near the mouth of streams entering a lake or in the shallow areas of tributaries. They do on occasion spawn in sandy, gravelly areas but your best bet by far is to stay around brush piles, stumps, lily pads, weeds, willows or most any type of cover.

You will frequently find that it is almost too easy to locate big crappie by fishing such covers and staying around the brush piles. Drop your jig or minnow right on the spawning beds and you can catch them anytime during the day.

Don't worry if you pull in a few females during spawning season. Each female crappie will lay from 10 to 20 thousand eggs and the big majority of them will hatch. It is highly unlikely that you will overfish a crappie bed, in fact, biologists claim that such fishing actually helps the crappie population rather than hurts it.

The exact time of crappie spawning will vary in different parts of the country by a few months depending on what part of the country you live in. It may be well to check with local crappie fishermen in a given area to find out when the crappie spawning season normally runs. It obviously would start a lot sooner in Florida than in New York, varying as much as January in the South to early July in the North.

Even this information could only be used as a guideline for a late spell of freezing weather could delay the spawning. A more reliable method would be to purchase a good thermometer. This is one of the best investments a fisherman can make. If you know the temperature of the water and you know the temperatures at which various fish like to feed, you can save yourself many a dry run. Regarding the crappie spawning season, we want to remember water temperature ranging from 64 to 68 degrees from 2 to 7 feet deep. This is extremely important if we hope for large crappie catches during the spring season. A little later, we will discuss temperature feeding in greater detail.

As a general guideline, you may refer to the following states as representative of when the crappie spawning normally occurs.

> Florida—January through March
> Mississippi—Around March
> Oklahoma—usually around April
> Tennessee-Kentucky—Late March through April
> Ohio—Usually May or June
> Iowa-Nebraska—Late April and May
> New York—From late May to early July

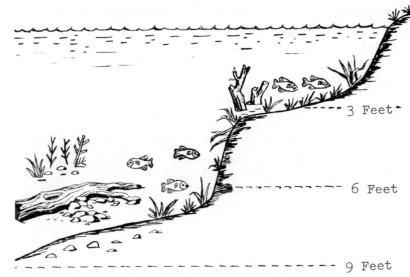

--- 3 Feet

--- 6 Feet

--- 9 Feet

During the spring season, crappies will spawn in waters of 2 to 7 feet deep. It is almost too easy to catch big crappie during this period by locating spawning beds around brush piles, stumps and other underwater cover.

One excellent method for locating crappie beds during spawning season is to use a small jig with a small silver spinning blade. Always keep the lures small. Crappie will occasionally hit a large lure but not often. They definitely prefer the smaller ones. Toss your spinning jig into an area that might contain spawning crappie. Let the lure sink all the way to the bottom, then raise it just off the bottom and jig it up and down. If there are any crappie near by you will soon know it because they cannot resist hitting a small spinning jig fished in the proper manner. If you don't get a bite after five or six such efforts, you might as well move to another area.

Continue this procedure until you start taking crappies. When they start biting, you know you have found their spawning beds.

When fishing for crappie during spawning season, you may find that you had a fabulous fishing trip one day only to return to the same spawning beds the next day and not get a bite. When this happens, check the water temperature. Often times, if the water drops a couple or three degrees, the crappie will move off the beds for a short spell. They rarely move far, just out to slightly deeper water and usually return in a few hours.

CHAPTER 3
LATE SPRING

After the crappies come off the spawning beds and while the water is still rather cool, under 72 degrees, they start cruising around the lake searching for food. Often they will move into bays and around the shoreline feeding in the late afternoon. This is an excellent time to use shallow-running spinning lures and also the fly-rod.

CHAPTER 4
SUMMER

After warm weather arrives, the crappies break up into small schools and move out into deeper water. They will either cruise around individually or in schools of ten to fifteen fish. They now become more difficult to locate and this is when many fishermen lay aside their rods until the following year. However, the crappies are still there, they will still bite, all you need do is find them. There are methods by which this can be done so the serious crappie fisherman need not put away his fishing tackle.

Because crappies are carnivores, devouring shad and minnows which they follow from place to place, they may be in one part of a lake one week and in a completely different part the next week. This can cause considerable frustration to the crappie fisherman because an area that produced fantastic results one week, may not produce a thing the next. However, this is part of the sport and a definite challenge to the crappie fisherman.

As you move further into the summer, the crappies move out deeper and deeper. They sometimes move into shallow bays and along shorelines in the evening and night but during the day may cruise in 20 to 25 feet of water. Even in summer, a good place to start looking for crappies is around trees sticking out of deep water. Drowned willows, sunken logs or any large cover objects are good bets as long as they are in deep water.

When fishing for crappie around deep water objects in hot weather, fish close to the bottom. Jigs or live minnows are usually considered best but they will also hit spinners and spoons.

During the late evenings and into the night of summer months, crappies usually move toward the surface. This is an excellent time to be on the water. Move around the lake quietly, watching for signs of crappie feeding. It is normally quite easy to locate a school or two at this hour if you are on a respectable crappie lake. If you can get close to the school without spooking them, you can reel them in about as fast as you can cast your lure.

If you fail to find crappies around shore cover, the next most popular hot- weather method is to try drifting with the wind across an open lake trying to locate a school of crappies. If you should catch a crappie, anchor quickly and continue fishing until they stop biting. Crappie most often travel in schools and when one is caught, you are usually in for some exciting fishing.

When you hit a school of crappies, the action is usually furious for awhile, then it stops abruptly. This means the school has moved out of range. Your best bet now is to move your boat upwind and start drifting through the general area again trying to relocate the same school. Or you may try casting around in a circle to find which direction the school is moving. If you can follow a school for any distance at all, you should soon have your limit.

Many successful crappie fishermen carry a small marker buoy with them. One could easily be made from a piece of styrofoam from any old ice chest or anything that will float. You would also need a bell sinker attached to a line which would easily unwind when you tossed the buoy into the water. Once the sinker hits bottom, it would hold the buoy in place. As soon as you catch a crappie while drift fishing, you should immediately toss the buoy into the water to mark the spot. The buoy would

One of the old time tactics for following a school of crappie was to first catch a crappie, then attach a line to it which was in turn attached to a balloon or bobber. By returning the crappie to the water, you simply followed the balloon or bobber as he led you to the school. Be sure to check your state laws before trying this as it is illegal in some states.

serve as a bearing to determine which direction the school is moving.

Since crappie normally travel in schools, you can increase your catch considerably by using a spreader with several hooks on the same line. It is not unusual to catch two crappies at the same time.

A final point about drift fishing for crappies is that it works primarily only in the summer and fall months. There is no point at all in drift fishing for crappie during the spawning season for, as we have already pointed out, they will be in near the shore. It is very important that you keep in mind the seasonal movement patterns of the crappie for you must go where he is, if you hope to catch him.

We will have more to say on summer fishing a little later under various topics regarding methods and techniques for catching crappie.

CHAPTER 5
FALL

In the fall as the waters start to cool, the crappie increases his activities and can once again be found all over the lake. During this period, they can be found in shallow as well as deep water.

Normally, crappies don't surface feed on insects in the fall but you can still find schools chasing shad or minnows. Streamer flies, spoons and spinners provide excellent fishing at this time.

Later in the fall when the water cools below 60 degrees, crappie retreat to deep water again. Jigs or live bait fished just off the bottom are now your best baits.

One excellent method for catching crappies in the fall is to find a lake with an irregular bottom that has various depressions or cavities. Crappies like to congregate in these depressions and especially so if the depression is located in an open pocket of a weed bed. In shallow water these depressions could be found with an oar, but in deeper water you would need an electronic depth finder.

Often you can pull from 7 to 10 crappies out of a single depression. Once you find a depression that produces, be sure to mark it for it will only be a question of time until more crappies move in and you can return to your 'private hole' for repeated action at other times.

CHAPTER 6
WINTER

Crappies can be caught during the winter months just as surely as they can be caught during any other time of the year. Again, you need only to know where he is at. When the water starts to really get cold, the crappie moves out into water normally 20 to 30 feet deep. They still concentrate in schools, usually in areas with stumps, brush or other debris.

If you live up north where the ice gets thick enough to support your weight, you can have an excellent time ice fishing for crappie. Minnows and various types of larvae seem to be the most popular bait with most fishermen, however, there are still many fishermen that will swear by the ice fly and jigging spoons. Fish close to the bottom in water around 20 to 30 feet deep. Crappies also bite well at night for the ice fisherman when fishing by the light of a gasoline lantern. They are apparently attracted to the light and will bite all night long.

If you live in the mid to lower states, winter fishing for crappies can still be a very rewarding experience even though there is no ice. First, you need to bundle up like an Eskimo for it can get mighty cold in a small boat on a big lake. But if you can tolerate this aspect of it, you can bring in some fine stringers.

Down in Western Kentucky, crappie fishermen have found that fine strings of crappies can be caught in December, January and February which you normally don't think of as fishing months. It is not unusual to see a group of fishermen come in from a day on the lake with full stringers of crappie. From all indications the secret is very simple--know the right depth at which crappies stay during the frigid months. The same rule of thumb applies here as to ice fishing--fish close to the bottom in water about 20 to 30 feet deep.

In searching for this area, just remember that crappies like to stay close to the bottom in the winter. Once you find the area, and if you can brave the weather, you will be in for some fine winter catches of crappie. I would strongly urge that once you hit the jackpot, that you mark the spot by taking a bearing on 3

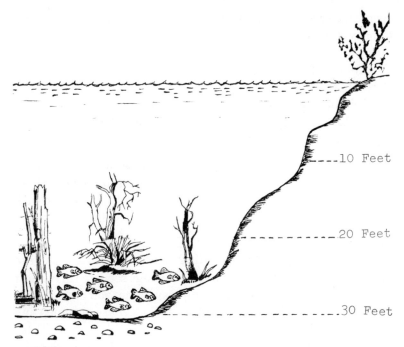

10 Feet

20 Feet

30 Feet

WINTER HABITAT - Once the water becomes quite cold, crappies will normally be found along the lake floor in 20 to 30 feet of water. Whether you are fishing through the ice or in open water, this is the depth at which you are most likely to catch crappie. Always look for underwater debris, sunken logs, drowned trees, etc.

SUMMER HABITAT - In the extreme hot months of summer, when the crappie are not cruising around the lake chasing shad and minnows, they will more than likely be found at about the same depth of the extreme winter months, in 20 to 25 feet of water, close to the bottom usually around underwater debris.

or 4 shoreline objects. You can be reasonably assured that in this area which the crappies have found most comfortable, that others will probably be in that same area in the following winter seasons.

During winter fishing, if you had been at a spot for a half hour or so with no bites, you should consider moving to another spot. Since crappie stay in schools, they sometimes remain stationary and you may be in the wrong place. If they have been biting but have suddenly quit, the school has probably moved off. You are now faced with the decision of whether to move or wait until another school comes along. Since the crappies were biting, it indicates you were at a spot which the crappies had found acceptable and your chances are probably best if you just wait at that same spot.

Crappies will often congregate in winter months near the mouth of a river or stream where it empties into the lake. They are attracted to the warmer waters flowing in so if you have such a water inlet in your fishing area, be sure to take a crack at it during the next winter season.

One final thought regarding winter activities. During those cold frigid months, germs and flu bugs seem to thrive best in our nice warm houses. So, if you stay home, you are going to catch the flu anyway. You might as well go chase crappies and enjoy yourself.

CHAPTER 7
NIGHT FISHING FOR CRAPPIES

Night fishing for crappies is becoming a big sport in many areas of the country. In fact, many crappie fishermen will tell you that if you want to really catch the big ones, there's only one sure way and that's by lantern light at night.

There seems to be some confusion as to why it works, but it is an established fact that you can take a lighted gasoline or propane lantern, place it on a dock or on a boat in deep water and within two hours, there will be crappies in the area by the hundreds.

Why the crappies are attracted to the light is not certain. Perhaps they are after the thousands of insects that are soon swarming around the light. Possibly minnows are after the insects and the crappies are after the minnows. Then maybe the crappies are just plain curious. Whatever the reason, it's an absolute certainty that crappies will congregate around a lighted lantern at night and just as they do during the day, they will gobble up anything in sight. If you haven't tried night time crappie fishing, you are missing a most enjoyable experience.

No specialized equipment is needed other than a lantern, however there is almost no end to the gadgets you can buy if you really want to go first class. Most authorities recommend a gasoline or propane lantern, preferably the double mantle versions as they give off more light, however a single mantle is quite adequate. Kerosene lanterns are normally not recommended as they don't have the brightness of the other two.

The only requirement is that the light be bright. If you are around a dock where there is electricity, a flood or spotlight dangling over the water will work fine.

If you are fishing from a boat, you might want to consider a reflector on the lantern to keep the glare out of your eyes. Some anglers have been known to use old garbage can lids as reflectors by painting the underside white. Other items might include a small stove for fresh coffee or stools with heaters for cool nights.

In some areas they have made night fishing a year-round, first class luxury. Old barges have been enclosed, and for a fee, you can fish from a heated room in winter, or air conditioned in the summer. A few are so elaborate as to include carpeting, color TV, lounge seats and a snack bar.

For night fishing, the minnow is probably most popular, however, in an area where mayflies abound, you can bait your hook with them with good results. Artificials will also take crappies at night. White and yellow colored jigs or jig-flies are quite effective as are small spinners and streamers. When worked in the lantern's light, they will often outproduce the natural baits.

Although night fishing is normally limited to spring and summer, it needn't be so. The fish don't leave. They're still there and feeding throughout the year and there is no reason why night fishing for crappie cannot be a year- round affair.

Night fishing for crappies can add a new dimension to your angling enjoyment. If you haven't tried it, I strongly recommend that you try to work in a night on the lake at your first opportunity.

One can easily locate or build his own 'private crappie hole' that will be good for fine catches of crappie year after year. I am not recommending that you sink your boat as the illustration might imply, but you can sink old auto frames, Christmas trees, logs, etc. Crappies love to congregate around most any kind of underwater debris.

CHAPTER 8
TEMPERATURE

One of the most important aspects of becoming a successful crappie fisherman is to understand water temperatures and know how to interpret them. This statement would also apply when going after any species of fish.

All fish have what we will refer to as an active feeding temperature range. In the case of the crappie, their active feeding range is when the water temperature is between 65 to 74 degrees F.

However, please note, their peak feeding temperature is around 71 degrees F. Obviously, we will want to search for water at around 71 degrees for top action. A few degrees, one way or the other, will greatly reduce their feeding activities.

An underwater thermometer is one of the most important investments a serious fisherman can make. Although a thermometer can't tell you how to fish, it can tell you the preferred water level at which your particular species is most likely to be.

As an example, during the normally hot months of July and August when many would-be-fishermen are on the sidelines due to the fish not biting, the temperature-oriented fisherman is having a ball. He knows that by taking temperature reading at various water levels, he need only search until he finds the preferred level for the species he is after. Often, this will mean fishing in water 20 to 30 feet deep. By applying this one principle, summer fishing can be just as exciting as any other time of the year.

At the risk of over-simplification, let us quickly go through a testing procedure. We move out into the shallow area of a lake and drop our thermometer to a depth of 5 feet, holding it there long enough to get an accurate reading. We find the temperature at this depth to be 80 degrees F. so we know the fish will not be biting at this level for it is too warm. We move further out into the lake and take a reading at a depth of 25 feet and find the temperature at this level to be 70 degrees F. This is the depth we want. Our best bet now is to find an area in the lake where we can hit bottom at a depth of 25 feet. You are now in the area where crappie are most likely to be--close to the bottom in their preferred temperature feeding range.

One point to keep in mind, you normally won't catch many crappies during the summer months in lakes which have a depth of less than 15 feet. These shallow lakes usually get too warm and the crappie simply stop feeding.

You should seek out the larger, deeper lakes and then

search for the crappie's preferred feeding temperature range of 65 to 74 degrees. Frequently, the temperature range will cover several feet in depth. The ideal situation is when the bottom level of your temperature range is around weed beds or other cover for this is where Mr. Crappie is most likely to be.

As we move into the winter season and the waters start to cool below the crappie's active feeding range, they will start to reduce their intake of food. All fish follow this same pattern. However, crappies can still be caught, even through ice, but we need to make adjustments in our fishing techniques.

Under cold water conditions, the crappie's metabolism becomes sluggish. The same situation exists when the water is too warm. Under both situations, we need to follow two rules. First, fish close to the bottom using a small lure or bait. They simply won't look at the big lures or bait, much less take them.

Unfortunately, they won't go very far out of their way for the small ones either, which brings us to rule No. 2. In very cold or very warm water, you must put your small lure or bait as close to the fish as possible. No trolling or casting for they will not chase it. Make it as easy for the fish as possible by driftfishing or stillfishing, and hopefully, putting your small lure or bait up close to the fish's mouth.

If you want to double your fishing action, don't overlook the technique of temperature fishing. It can often save you from getting skunked and add greatly to your fishing pleasure.

There are several thermometers on the market for fishermen and they vary from the sophisticated battery-operated devices with dial indicators to the simple old time mercury units. In using your thermometer, the important thing to remember is to be sure to take enough time to allow the sensor or mercury to adjust to a particular water level in order that you get an accurate reading.

CHAPTER 9
BUILD YOUR OWN
PRIVATE CRAPPIE HOLE

If you live on a lake or have access to one, it is very easy to build your own private crappie hole. In the hot summer months, at a spot where the lake bottom temperature is 65 to 74 degrees,you can sink Christmas trees weighted with concrete blocks, old automobile frames, logs, brush piles or most any type of junk and you will have almost instant fishing.Be sure to mark your spot by sighting in on 3 or 4 shoreline objects. You can return all summer long (and every summer) to your private crappie hole for almost certain strings of crappie.

As an example of how effective this can be, a family in Wisconsin has reported they always camp at the same lake each summer. They state they are never without crappie for they had located a boat that had sunk in about 25 feet of water. They would return to the boat each summer and crappie would always be swarming around the place.

For spring fishing, you would want to build your 'private crappie hole' in the more shallow areas where the crappie spawn.

If you like to night fish, here is a surefire formula for building your own crappie hole in which the crappies will come to you. Find an appropriate spot, then take some bales of alfalfa, discarded Christmas trees or cottonseed cake. All are equally effective. The theory is that these items attract small organisms which in turn attract the minnows which in turn attract crappies. When you add the bright lights which we have already discussed under Night Fishing, you are surely set for some hot action. Don't be surprised if you pull in a few bass and catfish along with the crappies.

Regarding the sunken boat I referred to a couple of paragraphs ago, a similar incident occurred involving old junker automobiles. A few years back, the folks in Hawaii found themselves with a few thousand abandoned cars that were rusting and creating unsightly conditions around the countryside.

Since there were no recycling facilities at the time, they finally hit on the solution of depositing the cars on the ocean floor. It turned out to be a bonanza for the local fishermen. The cars provided a place for the recently hatched fish to hide from voracious larger fish, which in turn attracted even larger fish. The Division of Game and Fish reported that in the area of the sunken automobiles, the fish population increased 4000 percent in six years. Which is another way of saying that whether it is crappie or most any other fish, they like to congregate around any kind of obstacles that provided them with shelter and a place to hide.

One of the most successful man-made crappie attractions that I have read about was located on Kentucky Lake. One of the dock owners learned that by pounding long stakes into the lake bottom to form a crib, that it attracted crappie in unbelievable numbers. So much so, that the dock owner would guarantee his customers plenty of crappie action on a year round basis.

To the crappie, the cribs somewhat resembled an old fort like the ones our forefathers built in pioneer days. The stakes were simply driven into the lake bottom to form a big square or rectangle. He would then place a heavy weight in the center of the crib, tie a line to it with a bobber or some floating object to be used as a marker.

The crappies loved it. They would gather around the cribs rubbing their sides on the wooden slats waiting for one of the many minnows that also were attracted to the object. The beauty of his system was that you might catch all the crappie around a crib one day, return a day or two later and have another ball as a new supply of crappie had moved in.

One group of six fishermen reported catching 400 crappies in two hours when fishing the cribs. The nice thing about it, there were no hang-ups when fishing around the smooth sided stakes as you might experience when fishing around brush piles or other debris.

While on the subject of hang-ups, as a serious crappie fisherman, you will be almost certain to experience a good many of these unpleasant encounters. That is because crappie so frequently hole up around brush piles, submerged logs and other objects which are so easy to snag.

Fortunately, there is a simple solution. Use thin-wire Aberdeen hooks. When you experience a hang-up, rather than drop a bait retriever down your line to disengage the hook which will create quite a commotion and spook the fish, you simply pull the aberdeen hook free. Since they are thin-wire, the hook easily straightens out and comes free. A pair of pliers can quickly be used to bend the hook back to its original and proper shape.

CHAPTER 10
BANK FISHING vs BOAT FISHING

Like most other aspects of living, a fisherman must face the facts of life and if you fish for crappie from the banks, the odds are stacked against you. This is not to say they can't be caught from the bank. As a youngster growing up in Kentucky, I caught many a crappie from the banks of Slate Creek and from a small farm lake known as Jess Highland's pond.

If you must fish from the bank, follow the same instructions already discussed by fishing around weed beds, sunken logs and other cover. However, it should be understood that fish usually do not come to you. You must seek out the fish by knowing something of his habitat, his feeding habits, his preferred water temperature, etc. This normally requires a boat for maximum success.

CHAPTER 11
FINDING THE BEST CRAPPIE LAKES

Most of the dollars I've earned in my life were made as a salesman and I learned a long time ago that if a salesman wants to find out something about his prospect or his needs, the best way is to ask a lot of questions. The same thing applies to finding good crappie lakes. Don't hesitate to ask the local tackle dealers, conservation officers, fishing editors of local newspapers, radio or TV. If you have some extra change, you may want to hire a guide the first time on a new lake.

A point to keep in mind is that crappies fluctuate in size from lake to lake. Some lakes grow jumbo crappies, whereas other lakes seem to produce crappies that are stunted. In searching for the better lakes, try to find one that has a record of producing big crappies in recent years.

How do we determine what is a big crappie? When the crappie is about two years old, he normally weighs about one pound. Most fishermen consider this to be a good size crappie. However, in good crappie waters, they will hit weights of around 3 pounds by their 3rd or 4th year and measure out at 15 inches. Crappies have been caught at weights exceeding 5 pounds.

Crappies have a paper-thin mouth and should be taken from the water by net. The weight of a good size crappie can often tear the hook from his mouth and away he goes.

CHAPTER 12
ELECTRONIC DEPTH
AND FISH FINDER

We mentioned earlier that a thermometer is one of the best investments a fisherman can make. If you still have any fishing money left over by now, you may want to consider an electronic fish finder or depth finder. These can be an invaluable aid in locating schools of crappie when they are suspended in deep water during months other then spawning season. It could also be used to locate deep depressions or irregular bottoms, underwater forest, brush piles or other cover areas where crappies like to stay.

The electronic depth finder, combined with the underwater thermometer are becoming required tools of trade for the professional fisherman, if he hopes to stray abreast of his fellow professional anglers. By using the thermometer to find the depth of the preferred water temperature for the species you are seeking, then using the electronic depth finder to find bottom at the desired water temperature, many fishermen are finding it almost too easy to take the limit.

One top professional bass fisherman who has perfected this technique recently took 35 bass in 1 1/2 hours using the thermometer and depth finder method. At last count, he had won eleven major bass fishing tournaments. This same technique is equally effective for crappies.

CHAPTER 13
TACTICS FOR CATCHING CRAPPIE

Practically every tactic imaginable has been tried at one time or another for catching crappie. I am not saying they all work all the time but I'll list a few of them for whatever value you want to give them.

One story involves an old timer who used to always catch more crappies than his fellow fishermen. Under pressure from his buddies, he finally divulged his secret. Before baiting his hook, he would trim the marginal fin of his minnow. This made the minnow appear more livelier for it had to swim more vigorously in order to get around. His minnow, being more active, attracted more crappies, at least this was his explanation for his success.

Another story involves the fisherman who took a gallon jar, filled it with water, added a couple of dozen minnows and covered the opening with a piece of thin cloth. He then lowered it next to a brush pile and left it for a few hours. When he returned, so he claimed, the crappies would be there, ready and willing, having worked up a ravaging appetite trying to get at the minnows inside the jar.

A slight variation but somewhat related story involves the selection of a good looking crappie spot and them bait it for several days with cottonseed cake. As the cottonseed cake slowly dissolves, it will attract schools of minnows which, in turn, will attract schools of crappie.

As we have already mentioned, crappies travel in schools and they eat almost continuously. Once they devour all the food in one area, they move on to another and keep eating and moving.

One of the old tricks of attracting the roving schools of crappie to your area is to make a noise that imitates the sound of a school of crappies churning the surface chasing minnows.

Here are a few of the things that various fishermen have used to simulate that sound.

One old timer uses a large bass lure with a spinner at both ends. He has it tied to a short pole and just pulls it back and forth in the water to create a commotion.

Another simply beats the water around his boat with a long cane pole.

Still another takes a boat paddle and ripples it through the water with slashing, slurping strokes.

Then there is another that takes his electric motor, turns it on low speed, then angles the propeller so it churns the surface of the water.

There is almost no limit to the tactics that have been used to attract crappies. One fellow has devised a system where he rolls up two paper wads out of wax paper. He then puts a strong rubber band around the two wads of paper and starts twisting until there is considerable tension on the rubber band. He then bounds the wads with a strip of water soluble tape and would toss it among a batch of lily pads. The wax paper would float until the tape became soaked and came loose. The wads would then jump and dance around as the tension of the rubber band caused it to unwind. If there were any crappies in the area, they came to investigate and it was reported the old fellow caught many of a whopper size crappie using this technique.

There is still another method that has been used for locating schools of crappie. I an not saying I recommend it but I will list it nevertheless. First, you must catch a crappie. Then you attach a line to the crappie which has attached to the other end, an inflated balloon. Since crappies travel in schools, you simply return your lone crappie to the water then follow the bouncing balloon as he leads you to the nearest school of crappie. However, before trying this, be sure to check your state laws. It may be illegal in some states.

Another tactic you might consider is when the water temperatures close to shore are in the crappie's preferred temperature range, crappies will occasionally feed very near the shoreline, especially in grassy areas. You can sometimes move your boat along the edge of the grassy areas, then go back and fish the water which you have just disturbed. As your boat disrupts the grass, you are knocking various types of insects from the grass into the water. This will often start the crappie to feeding. Although this trick won't work every time, successful crappie fishermen have reported it working on several occasions.

Still another technique for taking crappie is to be observant. If you see a couple of fishermen pulling in large quantities of crappie from a certain spot, make a mental note of it. It may be a little sneaky but the next morning make sure you are anchored at that same spot at the break of daylight.

In developing techniques for taking crappie, some unusual storied have occurred. For example, there is an old country expression, "Well, that sure tore the rag off the bush." It has been said the expression originated from crappie fishermen who would tie a rag on to a tree limb or bush to mark the spot where they had caught several nice crappies. It was considered a truly rotten trick to remove one of the rags which would prevent the fisherman from returning to his favorite crappie hang-out.

One last story involved the pioneers of early Kentucky. They discovered the crappie in some of the Kentucky streams and being unfamiliar with the species, named them "new lights." At the same time, there was a religious group flourishing in Kentucky called the Campbellities and they too, along with the crappie were referred to as "new lights." There are many sections in Kentucky where the crappie is still called "new lights."

Here are a few points to remember that can often make the difference between going home empty handed or with a full stringer.

In approaching your fishing spot, do so as quietly as possible. Avoid all unnecessary noises. Crappies are easily spooked, as are most fish, especially the larger one. Try to avoid scraping or thumping the bottom of your boat and row quietly. When walking along the bank of a lake or stream, walk lightly and try to avoid having your shadow fall across the area you intend to fish. When dropping anchor, do so quietly, and avoid loud talking or shouting, as loud voices will carry into the water. To summarize, if the crappies don't know you're there, you stand a better chance of catching more and bigger ones.

CHAPTER 14
CATCHING BIG CRAPPIE

In catching crappies, big or small, always remember that the crappie has a soft, paper thin mouth. If you set the hook too hard, you can tear or jerk it right through his mouth. Crappies seldom bang your bait as some other species, but rather seem to suck it in slowly and then head for the deep. Just be careful that you don't set the hook too hard.

Also, if you hook a big one, be careful in trying to hoist him into a boat. His weight can often tear the hook right through his mouth and away he goes. It is best to use a landing net or lead the crappie along side your boat and slip your finger beneath his gill in order to lift him from the water.

CHAPTER 15
MUDDY WATER

It will be well to remember that crappie do not hit in muddy water and there is no point in wasting your time when the water is in this condition. Also, when high winds are lashing against the shorelines, it scares the crappie and they move into deeper water. When this condition exists, you obviously won't want to fish near the shores.

CHAPTER 16
BAITS & LURES FOR CRAPPIE

Trying to determine the most effective bait or lure used to catch crappies would be an almost impossible task. Many fishermen swear by the minnow but there is almost certainly an equal number that swear by the jig or some other lure. One thing that is very definite is that crappies will hit almost anything if presented at the proper time in the proper manner; minnows, crickets, flies, streamers, jigs, popping bugs, spinners, spoons and plugs. You name it and a crappie has probably taken it at one time or another. They have even been known to take bare treble hooks with only a small pork rind attached, and it's been said, they've been caught with only a rag attached to the hook.

In attaching the minnow to your hook, four methods seem to prevail. One, put the hook through the lips of the minnow being careful not to damage his brain or you kill the minnow. Two, hook the minnow through the back but keep it shallow in order that you don't damage the spine which is also fatal. Three, insert the hook through the meat of the tail. And four, you might try hooking the minnow through both eyes. He will still stay lively and won't be as easy to get off the hook. Try each method and determine which seems best for you.

On a par in popularity with minnows would be the jigs and jig-flys. One of the best crappie fisherman I ever met was a fellow named Byron Leonard from Tennessee. I visited with him the day after Thanksgiving in 1969 and he had just returned from an afternoon of fishing with three other fellows. As I recall, his three companions had been using minnows and had not caught a single crappie. Mr. Leonard had been using a white jig-fly tied on a No. 8 hook and he had caught ten crappies. I saw five of them (the other five he had given to his buddies), and they were all whoppers. I don't believe a single one would have weighed in under 3 pounds. He makes the jig-fly himself from a mold which he made from a pair of pliers. He claimed that he had been catching them like that for 25 years.

Jig-Fly #10 Hook

Jig-Fly #6 Hook

When fishing jigs, jig-flys or jigging spoons, lower the lure to the bottom, then give it a slight wiggle and jig it up and down slowly. As you bring it slowly to the surface, give it various sorts of gentle twists. It is this movement of the lures which the crappie find so irresistible.

In addition to using live minnows and jigs, you will also find that when the crappies are in deep water, that small weighted spinners, small spoons and tiny, wiggling, running plugs can be effective.

When the crappie are feeding on the surface, popping bugs, streamers and flies are your best bet.

It is recommended that you use a light, limber rod as this can be helpful in your effort to avoid tearing the crappie's tender, tissue-thin mouth.

Regarding the test line, when using very light lures or baits without bobbers or sinkers, it is almost essential to stay with a 2 to 4 lb. test line in order to get a decent cast. As you move into heavier lures or baits with bobber and sinker, you can switch to the stronger test lines.

When fishing with lures, it should be of interest to note that crappie have been taken on just about every color in existence, however, without much doubt, white and yellow are the most popular two colors among the majority of fishermen with green and black being pretty much tied for third and fourth.

You should also remember that if your lure has a spinning blade, make sure it is a blade that spins when retrieved very slowly. Many blades are designed so they do not spin unless retrieved rapidly. This is not the way to fish for crappie. You want your lure to move slowly to be an effective crappie lure.

CHAPTER 17
RODS, REELS & CANE POLES

Several years ago, the most popular item for taking crappies was the cane or bamboo pole. In recent years, however, it has been replaced by various spincasting outfits. The reason is obvious. The majority of the spincasting reels now being sold can be operated trouble-free by the most inexperienced of fishermen. And it's more fun. A one pound crappie hooked to a light spincasting outfit can put up an interesting and creditable fight, something he was incapable of doing against the bamboo pole.

In selecting a spincasting outfit exclusively for crappie fishing (and also for other panfish), it is suggested that you select ultra-light tackle for maximum fishing enjoyment. A light, limber rod weighing about 2 or 3 ounces with a reel weighing about 6 or 7 ounces and a monofilament line ranging form 2 to 4 pound test is recommended. An ultra-light outfit offers at least 3 advantages: (1) you can cast extremely small lures, down to 1/32 of an ounce, (2) since it doesn't weigh much, you can fish for hours without getting tired and (3) when you hook a one pound crappie, he feels like a monster. You can get every bit as much enjoyment out of playing a small fish on such an outfit as you would in catching a fat bass on heavy tackle.

CHAPTER 18
DESCRIPTION OF THE CRAPPIE

There are two different species of crappie; the white crappie (Pomoxis annularis) and the black crappie (Pomoxis nigromaculatus). The two fish closely resemble each other and it is sometimes difficult to tell them apart from appearance alone. They are referred to by many names such as calico bass, speckled perch, specs, etc. It is sometimes spelled croppie and other times crappie. I've also heard it pronounced both ways as the spelling would indicate.

As the names imply, one is usually of a darker color, whereas the other is more silvery color. However, color alone is not always a reliable means of identification. Best bet is to count the stiff spines in the dorsal fin; if it's 7 or 8, you usually have a black crappie; it it's 6, you probably have a white crappie.

The white is more common in the South while the black is stronger in the North. However, the white appears to be more prolific and can withstand adverse water conditions better than the black. In lakes where both fish are found, the whites eventually dominate the population. The long range trend appears to be toward a predominantly white crappie population.

CHAPTER 19
CLEANING THE CRAPPIE

Many crappie fishermen still use the old tried and proven method of scaling the fish, cut off the head, remove the entrails, then wash and fry. And there is not a thing wrong with it.

However, once a fish is 6 inches or longer (the majority of crappies you catch should exceed this), it is generally more desirable to fillet it. Contrary to popular opinion, filleting does not waste a lot of meat. When filleted properly, you will recover most of the edible part of the fish and you then have a piece of meat without bones that you can truly enjoy eating.

It is not difficult to fillet a crappie. First, lay the fish on a board an literally, you will slice one side of the fish from the carcass. Start about mid way of the fish on the topside by inserting the knife along one side of the backbone. Cut deeply into the flesh and stay as close to the backbone as possible, cutting toward the fish's head. Hold the fillet away from the fish as you cut.

Now come back to your starting point and start cutting toward the tail, again cutting along side and as close to the backbone as possible. Move the knife blade back and forth until the fillet has been cut free from the backbone and rib cage. Now turn the fish over and remove the fillet from the other side in the same manner, then throw away the remaining carcass.

It should be pointed out that by filleting in this manner, it was not necessary to remove the head, scales, fins or entrails.

You now have two fillets that requires one more step. Place the fillet, skin side down, on the cutting board. To skin the fillet, start cutting away the flesh from the skin. This can be done very easily by keeping the knife slanted toward the skin as you move the knife forward, Once you have skinned a few fillets in the is manner, you will find that one quick stroke of the knife quickly separates skin from the flesh. The skin, which still has the scales attached is thrown away, and your fillet is now ready to be washed and prepared for eating.

If you have never filleted crappies, you will soon find that it is faster than cleaning the whole fish, it is more pleasant (not having to clean out the entrails, etc.) and it makes for better eating as you will have no bones to contend with.

HOW TO FILLET A CRAPPIE

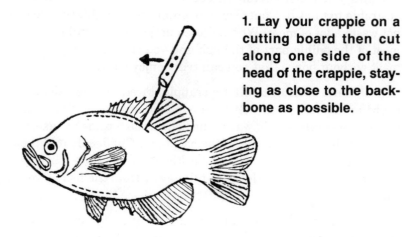

1. Lay your crappie on a cutting board then cut along one side of the head of the crappie, staying as close to the backbone as possible.

2. Return to original position and cut toward the tail, staying close to the backbone.

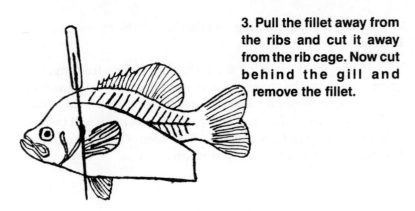

3. Pull the fillet away from the ribs and cut it away from the rib cage. Now cut behind the gill and remove the fillet.

4. Lay fillet on cutting board with skin down and cut the skin away from the flesh. Use a fork to hold the fillet if you wish.

CHAPTER 20
FREEZING

Crappies can easily be frozen and preserved for future use as the need arises. The main problem is to keep them from drying out. All fish have a tendency to dehydrate after a period of time in a freezer, especially if not properly wrapped. There are several ways this can be avoided. First, always freeze your fish as soon as possible after catching. Fish spoil quickly in warm weather, especially if they have not been cleaned.

One excellent method that will prevent dehydration and preserve your fish almost indefinitely is to put them in plastic containers, or any kind of a waterproof container, fill it with water and freeze the fish in a block of ice.

It is actually desirable to freeze the entire fish without cleaning or skinning. The skin and scales provide very good protection against dehydration. If you prefer not to freeze them in solid ice, then they should be wrapped tightly in a saran wrap or cellophane paper making certain that all the air possible has been squeezed out.

If you must clean or fillet the fish before freezing, you greatly increase the chance of dehydration and loss of some of its juicyness and flavor. By freezing the crappie whole, then thaw and clean or fillet when you are ready to cook it, he will taste as delicious as the day he was caught. One word of caution, never let fish thaw until you are ready to clean and use.

CHAPTER 21
RECIPES

The pleasures of crappie fishing can be divided into two distinct areas: catching them and then eating them. Without a doubt, the crappie is one of the best tasting fish to be found.

Probably the most popular method for cooking crappies is to roll them in flour or corn meal, fry to a golden brown and serve with hush puppies. If you don't care for the flour or corn meal, them simply fry them in melted butter or bacon grease. Before frying, you may wish to season with salt and pepper and possibly some onion or garlic salt.

If your crappie has been filleted, you should first dip it in milk or a whole beaten egg, then roll it in corn meal or cracker crumbs. If you like a thick batter, you should repeat the dip and roll procedure several times. When done, the batter will give the fillets a golden-brown color and it also prevents the fillets from drying out. They can either be pan fried or French fried (deep fried). Be sure that your fat is fresh and never rancid. Fry at a temperature of about 375 degrees F. until golden brown. Be careful that you don't overcook. This is a mistake that entirely too many people make---my wife, Ethel, being the first one that comes to my mind. Overcooking will greatly diminish the eating pleasure of crappie.

If you want to get fancy, here's a few other recipes you might try on your next catches of crappies.

Make a stuffing out of the following items: 1 cup of bread crumbs, 1 tablespoon of minced parsley, 1 tablespoon minced celery tops, 1 tablespoon minced onion, 1/2 teaspoon poultry seasoning, 2/3 cup of melted butter, salt and pepper to taste.

Now put the stuffing inside of a cleaned crappie and sew up the opening. Place in a buttered pan and bake in a moderately heated oven for about 25 minutes or until you can take a fork and flake the meat easily.

Here's another one. Take several crappie fillets and some slices of American cheese--about 3 parts fish to one part cheese. Roll the fillets in flour, then in a casserole dish add alternate layers of fillets and cheese. Pour in enough milk to barely cover the fillets and top it with a layer of Parmesan cheese. Bake at 350 degrees until the fillets are tender.

Here is one that even a Frenchman would like. Take several fillets and place them in a baking pan. Now add a can of undiluted mushroom soup. Be sure the soup covers the fillets but do not dilute the soup. Bake in an oven at 350 degrees until the fillets are tender.

If you're still game, you might try this one. Bake your crappies in aluminum foil until the meat flakes easily. Then take 2 1/2 cups of the flaked crappie meat along with 2 cups of cooked rice, 3 chopped hard-boiled eggs, 3 tablespoons chopped parsley, 3 tablespoons chopped pimento, 1/2 teaspoon of paprika, 1/2 cup of cream, salt and pepper to taste.

Mix the ingredients well and put into the top of a double boiler until it is steaming hot. Tastes fine on hot cornbread or toast.

For baked crappie, this is an excellent method. Take your whole cleaned crappie (no fillets), rub thoroughly with butter or margarine, salt and pepper to taste, wrap in aluminum foil and bake at 350 degrees until tender. Always preheat the oven before putting in the crappie.

Crappies can also be broiled quite satisfactorily. However, in cleaning the fish, remove only the scales and not the skin. The skin should be left intact as it will prevent drying out while cooking. Rub the crappie thoroughly with butter, salt and pepper to taste, then broil until tender. You should only turn it once while cooking. Serve with a slice of lemon if you wish.

If you are a chowder lover, this one is about as good as any.

Into a pan of water, cut up 6 medium size potatoes and 4 medium size onions into small pieces. Boil until done.

Add about 1 1/2 to 2 pounds of diced crappie fillets, then cook until the fillets are tender. Add 2 tablespoons of bacon fat and 3 tablespoons of butter. Add enough milk to make it as thick or thin as you wish. Heat slowly being careful not to boil the milk, add a little salt and pepper and it is ready to serve.

And here is a final one; crappie fillets, Polish style. You need 6 tablespoons butter, 1 cup fine bread crumbs, 8 crappie fillets, 6 white onions sliced very thin, salt and pepper, 1 1/2 sups sour cream and 2 tablespoons chopped fresh dill or dry dill weed.

Butter the sides and bottom of a bake dish and line it with the bread crumbs. Place alternate layers of fillets and onion slices in the dish. Season each layer with salt and pepper. Also cover each layer with sour cream sprinkled with dill. Your last layer should have a heavy coating of sour cream. Bake uncovered in a preheated oven at 350 degrees for half an hour, or until the top layer of sour cream is golden brown. Run a table knife around the pan to loosen the fish so that it can be lifted out as a loaf. Sprinkle a little more dill atop, cut in thick slices and serve.

Hush puppies and crappies make a fine combination. Although originating in the South, hush puppies are now finding increasing favor in the North and throughout the country. Hush puppies are easy to make and this recipe is a very good one. Take 2 cups of corn meal, one cup milk or water, 2 teaspoons baking powder, 1 finely diced onion, salt to taste. Mix and then form into small balls and fry until good and brown.

Although a few of the preceding recipes may not appeal to you, I would recommend that you try several, then stick with the ones you find most to your liking.

The real proof of crappie fishing is in the eating. If you haven't indulged in a savory meal of crappie, you still have a treat in store for you. Sink your choppers into a few of these tasty fellows and you just may become a believer in year-round crappie fishing.

SECRETS FOR TAKING
BIG BLUEGILLS

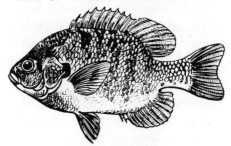

CHAPTER 1
THE BLUEGILL

Without question, the bluegill (Lepomis Macrochirus) is one of the most popular panfish in the United States. And for good reason. It is probably the most abundant and widely distributed fish in North America. It can be found in lakes, streams, government impoundments or farm ponds. In fact, it is actually difficult to find a sizeable body of fresh water that doesn't contain large quantities of bluegills. They can be caught every day of the year, in hot or cold weather and it doesn't make much difference if the sun is shining or if it's pouring down rain.

The bluegill is a spunky little fighter that will hit a fishing lure with gusto and then fight it out till the bitter end. Once hooked, he turns his broad side to the fisherman, then dashes back and forth, never giving up until he is landed. When caught on light fishing tackle, the bluegill can furnish you with plenty of thrills.

He is such a spirited little fighter that many fishermen have accused the bluegill of clinging to the water with claws. Others have said, jokingly I assume, that a one pound bluegill tied to a one pound trout would pull the trout inside out.

The bluegill are prolific breeders which account for their over abundance. In the spring, when they are in a loving mood, they will form a nest in which several females may deposit up to 60,000 eggs in a single nest. Most often, they nest in colonies with the nests sometimes so close, they practically touch each other. Can you just visualize a dozen or so nests, side by side, each one containing from 18,000 to 60,000 bluegill eggs? Is it any wonder the little scrapper is so abundant and is the favorite target of millions of fishermen from coast to coast. In fact, so abundant is the bluegill, that in many states the fisherman is urged to keep every bluegill he catches, regardless of size, in order that more food will be available for the balance of the population to prevent stunting.

Like most species, bluegills in the South usually attain larger average size than elsewhere due to the longer period of warmer weather. This allows the fish a greater growing season due to natural foods being available for longer periods of time. In areas of the Deep South, they have been caught up to a foot long and weighing over a pound. The world record was a 4 pound 12 ounce bluegill caught in Ketona Lake, Alabama in 1950. Just think of playing a bluegill of that size on a fly rod!

The bluegill is not choosy in trying to distinguish between the live bait fisherman or the artificial lure enthusiast. They will hit gaudy flies (wet or dry), popping bugs, nymphs, small streamers, weighted spinners or small spoons. On the live bait side, they will take a wide assortment of insects, larvae, nymphs, grubs and worms. They can be caught with equal ease on fly rods, spinning outfits or cane poles. To put it bluntly, the bluegill is not only a delightful battler, but he is downright obliging. This no doubt contributes to the bluegill being so popular with millions of fishermen when you consider that some of the other species are so finicky in their eating habits.

And last, but certainly not least by a long shot, the bluegill is a tasty little fellow. When fried to a crisp golden brown, he is down-right good eating that is just plain hard to beat.

There are many ways to fish for the bluegill and all of them will put fish on your table. However, the more you know about the bluegill, his habits and habitat, his natural foods, etc., the more of those eating size scrappers youll be able to sock away in the freezer. The following chapters are designed to give you that information.

CHAPTER 2
SPRING SPAWNING

The spring of the year is spawning time for the bluegill and it would be difficult to find a more productive, exciting or easier time to fill your stringer with the little scrappers. However, you will need to go more by water temperatures rather than the calendar, depending on which part of the country you live in. When the temperature reached 67 degrees F., it has hit the optimum water temperature for spawning of bluegills. This may be February or March in Florida, but June in Michigan and other northern states. You might refer to the following as representative spawning periods in various states.

Arkansas. . . . . Mid April to late June
Indiana . . . . Late May to late July. Peak period in June.
Minnesota . . . . . . Late May to early August. Peak in late June.
New York . . . . Early June to late August

If you are a real bluegill go-getter and want to be on the water at a peak fishing period, then be sure to remember this figure — 67 degrees F. If you don't own a small pocket thermometer, it would be highly advantageous to get one. It can pay for itself many times over. Don't be too concerned about the calendar date. Just keep tab on the water temperature. When it reaches 67 degrees F., crank up the old outboard motor. You won't find a better time for taking bluegills.

Usually the spawning season is spread out over several weeks or even a few months. Female bluegills will not all become ripe at the same time. She may deposit a batch of eggs and then a week later, make other deposits. This simply lengthens the spawning season and provides the fisherman with some extended shallow water fishing.

However, the evidence seems to suggest that the major part of the spawning occurs during the first two weeks of the season-- the first two weeks after the water reaches 67 degrees F., unless it is disrupted by a spell of high winds or cold weather. These two weeks will usually be your most productive fishing period.

Normally, the spawning beds occur at various water depths along the shoreline depending on the period of the spawning season. When the season first starts, the early spawning blue- gills move in close to shore in water one to three feet deep, normally on the lakes' north-northwest shore where they will get the greatest southern exposure to the sun. These are your first beds.

The next bedding will take place, still on the same side of the lake, but a little further out in four to six feet of water. As the water warms up, there is less need for direct sunlight and the bluegills now start bedding in the shallows of the south shore. This usually occurs about mid-way of the spawning season.

With continued warming, these beds will soon be deserted and you will need to look for new beds in six to ten feet of water. These are your last beds of the spawning season and they will quite often be found in the back areas of shaded coves which has a minimum of incoming water. It should be pointed out that these late, deep beds usually contain the largest nesting bulls.

There is hardly a more exciting time to take bluegills than while they are on the nest for they strike savagely during this period. They will not range far from the nest so your lures will have to be placed with precision, but when you are on target, be prepared for a vicious strike.

Perhaps you have hesitations about taking the gills while they are nesting. If so, by all means forget it. You will actually be doing your lake a favor with each one you pull out. It will mean that much more food for the remaining bluegills and with 18,000 to 60,000 eggs being deposited in each of those nests, you aren't likely to dent their population too greatly, if at all.

Where to find the nest? One of the differences between bluegills and other members of the sunfish family is that they like to nest in colonies. Often the nests practically touch each other with little separation between them.

Usually the nests are prepared on a clean sandy or gravel bottom in fairly shallow water. Most of the time they avoid weedbeds or areas where there is decaying vegetation on the bottom. In older ponds which has a soft muck bottom, look for an inlet stream where the current washes the bottom clean.

The nest is prepared by the male. He will hollow out a shallow depression from one to two feet in diameter and from two to six inches deep. He accomplishes this by violently swishing his tail and body. He then makes love to the female and persuades her to deposit her eggs in the nest, after which he covers them with milt to fertilize the eggs.

Bluegills have a tendency to return to the same spawning beds year after year. When the water is clear, you can often locate a bed visually on bright sunshiny days. A pair of good sunglasses will make this job easier. At night time, a powerful spotlight can be most helpful. Move your boat slowly over bottoms two to four feet deep and look for areas dotted with white oval spots about a foot or two in diameter. Sometimes you may find one with a diameter of eight to ten feet. These large ones were made by large males as they fanned the area clean of gravel and other debris.

The male keeps a constant guard over the nest and vigorously defends it against any and all intruders. He also keeps the eggs clean and aerated by the gentle fanning with his fins.

The hatching usually takes from two to five days if weather conditions are normal. After they are hatched, the male continues to protect the fry for a few additional days then he drives them toward cover and deserts them.

When to fish? This is a tough one. Many bluegillers will

argue that the best time is the first two and last two hours of daylight. However, I have personally experienced many an occasion, and probably every bluegiller can make the same statement, that at various times throughout the day, including high noon, the bluegills would hit almost as fast as you could get your line in the water. The time of day doesn't seem to be a critical factor when the water is at the right temperature, around 67 degrees F., and the gills are spawning.

What baits to use? Bluegills will hit such a wide assortment of live and artificial baits that we will deal with this as a later topic. However, during spawning season you might remember these points. Bluegill can occasionally be choosy. Perhaps it is due to the nest being in an area that is abundant with nymphs or other goodies. If the gills are not going for your bait, don't monkey around. Keep changing until you find the one that gets the action.

As I have already mentioned, the bluegills won't venture far from their nest and you must put the bait on target. If there is a swirl of water as your bait hits the surface, it means you have spooked the bull from the nest. Don't despair. He will always return within a few seconds. Let your bait sink and then very, very slowly ease it along just over the nest. As the spring season progresses, you will need to get your baits to settle deeper to attract the lunkers.

When the bluegills are on the beds, be on the lookout for swirls of water around the nest. This will usually mean a big bull is giving chase to some younger bluegills that cluster around the nest waiting for a chance to hijack a few eggs. You football fans will probably recall a Louisiana State team of a few years back that referred to one of their defensive units as the "Chinese Bandits." This would be am appropriate tag for these small bluegill. Not only have they cleaned the bait from many a fisherman's hook, but they are probably more of a pest to the nesting papa bluegill than to the fisherman by constantly trying to steal the eggs.

However, for a little icing on the cake, so to speak, next time you see those swirls of water, take out your favorite bass lure and start casting into the deeper water just outside the bluegill nest. Don't be surprised if you tie into an old cagey bass that was waiting for an opportunity to take some of those skittering little bluegills being chased away by the nesting bull.

To summarize spring fishing for bluegills, it's pretty much a matter of keep moving until you find them. There will be days when it seems that every shallow shore will contain an abundant supply of big bluegills that hit everything you toss at them. However, there will be other days when they are notoriously absent. If you can't find them and you are on a strange lake, it could well be worth your time to hire a local guide to show you where the good bluegill holes are at. One or two good holes could easily make it worth the price.

CHAPTER 3
SUMMER

When summer arrives and the water begins to really warm up, it will suddenly seem that the big bluegills have disappeared. Of course they haven't. Instead, they have moved away from their love making areas around the shallow shores and have headed into deeper, cooler water.

Where to find bluegill on hot summer days? By now the lake vegetation is at its peak which gives the bluegills more places to hide. Obviously, cover provides the bluegill with protection and comfort. In addition to this, it makes a nice hiding place in which he can dart out to snag minnows and other small food fishes. So in looking for the best summer spots to fish, the answer is always--where there is cover.

Some of their favor spots are around docks and piers which are on the edge of deep water. They will also congregate in offshore weed beds and among the long-stem lily pads. They can also be found in brush areas or along side dams and breakwaters. Be sure to check the steep structures out in the middle of the lake, such as reefs and shoals as they often contain large quantities of bluegills during the hot summer months. The deeper water just off rocky points and steep sloping shores can also be rewarding on occasions.

When to fish? Almost without question, the most productive hours during the summer are the first two hours of dawn and the last two hours just before dark. During the heat of day, the big bluegills move out into water 15 to 20 feet deep. They remain pretty much inactive throughout the day, especially on bright sunny days, but in the late evening they move back into the shallows to feast on night-flying insects. This is when your surface lures are most useful, such as dry flies, small poppers and rubber spiders.

There is an exception to summer mid-day fishing. On overcast days when the sun's bright rays have been blocked out, you can often catch bluegills throughout the entire day. If there is a light drizzle, they seem to bite that much better.

After a hard raining spell in which the lake has turned off color, an almost certain method for taking some fine bluegills is to find a trickle of clear water entering the head of a slough or cove. Toss your bug into the clear water and let the current take it under. This is one of the sure ways for taking a few big ones.

Another method is to start out from the shore in about ten feet of water. Fish the area but keep moving out into the deeper water just a foot or so at a time. As soon as you catch your first bluegill, you should promptly ease your anchor into the water and start fishing the immediate vicinity of where you made the catch. In fact, it is usually best to have two anchors, one at each end of the boat. This will lock the boat in place and prevent the wind from drifting the boat from your fishing spot. It is important that you stay in the exact area of your first catch. A few feet one way or the other and you may be out of range of the feeding area. Also, you should waste no time in getting your line back into the water. Bluegills will occasionally go into feeding sprees that last no longer than half an hour. You shouldn't have your line anyplace except in the water during one of those feeding sprees.

Toward mid-summer when the oxygen is at a low point,

bluegills often move into the turbulence below the dams and falls. It not only provides them with comfort but it is an excellent place for them to find food. Your spinning or spincast outfits are usually best for these areas. A very small, light weighted spinner or a mini-plug about one inch long can be effective. Sometimes, a short thin strip of pork rind attached to the spinner is helpful.

When fishing the deeper beds, 15 to 20 feet, it is usually best to attach a small split-shot sinker about 3 feet above your bug. You can fish without the sinker but be sure to allow adequate time for the bug to sink all the way to the bed. Then allow fairly lengthy intervals between twitches of your line. Best colors for the deep beds seem to lean toward green or brown. It should be noted that the deeper beds produce bigger bull bluegills than the shallow beds.

Drift fishing across an open lake can occasionally be an effective method for finding the big bluegills. Not only that, it's a nice, relaxing way to fish since you are letting the wind work for you. First, move to the upwind side of the lake at an angle to the wind that will give you the longest midlake drift possible. As you move across the lake you will actually be trolling except that you are being powered by the wind rather than a motor.

If you are drifting fast enough to keep a spinning blade in motion, then a small spinner is probably your best bet. Otherwise, live bait such as grasshoppers, crickets, small minnows or tiny crayfish may be your best offering.

As you slowly drift over the water with your bait just off the bottom, you can imagine the frequent foul ups you will encounter. One method which will greatly reduce this problem is to take a tiny bottle cork and attach it about 6 to 8 inches above the bait, then place your sinker about a foot ahead of the cork. The sinker should be just heavy enough to keep the bait down but no heavier. The cork, of course, keeps the bait from getting snagged on the bottom, at least in theory. When you see the line tighten out, it usually means that a fat bluegill is hanging on at the other end.

When you hook a fish, you should immediately drop anchor to stop the forward motion of the boat. As you reel in the fish you should be doing two things,. This may sound silly, but it can pay off in big dividends. First, count the number of turns that it takes you to reel in the fish. Later you will need to measure the length of line in a single turn. Let's say it was 6 inches, for convenience, and it took you 120 turns to boat the fish. This means your boat is 60 feet away from where you caught the fish.

Second, as you are reeling in the fish, you should be sighting in on the shore line. Pick out two objects--one immediately at the edge of the shore and another directly behind it but further inland. Now turn directly behind and do the same thing. You have now formed an imaginary line between 4 objects and you are setting squarely on top of it. Next, pull anchor, and start rowing along your imaginary line toward the spot that you caught the fish. When you covered the 60 feet, gently ease your anchor to the bottom and start having a ball.

It is conceivable that you will have latched onto a loner in which case your above efforts will have gone for nought. However, more than likely, since bluegills like to congregate in groups, you can usually expect to pull others from that same spot. Since this will be out in the deeper water, you can anticipate that these will be the larger size bulls that every fisherman dreams about.

The beauty of finding such a deep water hang out is that the big bluegills and their off-springs have formed a nice habit, that once they find a suitable spot in which the bottom has adequate cover for them to hide and which is also the right depth to contain the proper oxygen at a comfortable temperature, they will return to that spot year after year. So mark the spot well. Take 4 or 5 shore line sightings and you may well find that you now have your own little private bluegill hole that you can return to time after time for some nice catches.

One final point about summer fishing for bluegills, don't overlook those after dark hours. It's a most pleasant experience to be on the lake at night time and with any luck at all, you can usually tie into some real bragging size gills. We will have more to say on night fishing later.

CHAPTER 4
FALL

As the hot summer days slowly fade and autumn weather starts to move in, various changes in the water take place. The feeding habits of the bluegill change right along with it. The water temperature is becoming more comfortable and the fish become more active. They now have a tendency to bunch up in schools and roam the lake feeding on surface insects, zooplankton and algae.

It now becomes a matter of seeking them out. It is a period when the bluegill go on short feeding spurts and then drift into lulls where they are quite inactive.

Where to find them? In fall weather, you can often locate schools of bluegill by just being alert as you move around the lake. Watch for dimples on the water and listen for the telltale splash of the feeding gills as you roam the open water. Best lures for surface feeding are your dry flies, small poppers, spiders and streamers, mostly size 10.

During or after a light rain is an excellent time to try the tree lined coves as the steady drizzle has washed down food from the trees. During these all day drizzles is a highly desirable time to be on the lake for it is usually excellent bluegill fishing.

Fall weather often finds the bluegills swarming into rocky bottoms below dams and falls. If the water flow is light, they will usually be along the edge of the current, and if it is quite slow, sometimes they will be in it. If the current is fast, move to be backwash. Larva and insect baits or small minnows are usually best for this type of fishing. Also small jig-flies tied about three to four feet behind a plastic bubble are very effective.

The autumn season is also an excellent time to fish farm ponds and small lakes. Many of these smaller bodies of water are too shallow and simply become too warm during the summer. The fish become sluggish and feeding drops off next to nothing. But as fall weather brings on cooler and more comfortable water, their appetites take off. Unfortunately, in these shallow lakes under 15 feet deep, the same thing occurs in the winter. The water becomes too cold and the fish don't feed. I'm not sure if they are trying to make up for what they lost in the summer, or if they are just trying to store up a little fat for the winter, perhaps both; but no question, bluegill fishing in the fall months in shallow lakes can be good fishing.

While on the subject of farm ponds and small lakes, it should be noted that a fertile bluegill pond will produce approximately 200 pounds of fish per acre. Biologists estimate that at least 50 pounds or more of fish per acre should be removed each year from these farm ponds to keep the bluegill population in check. This means that most ponds could stand a lot more fishing pressure than they presently receive.

When to fish? The most productive time is still those early and later daylight hours. However, gills can be taken off and on throughout the day as they go in and out of those short feeding spurts. Don't overlook night fishing for autumn bluegills. It can be very productive.

CHAPTER 5
WINTER

Bluegills can be caught the year round, even in winter. Up North they can be taken through the ice, elsewhere in the open cold water. However, this is the toughest time of the year to take them, especially the big ones.

Where to find them? There's no set rule here except to go deep, usually in 10 to 20 feet of water and fish the bottom. Your chances are probably best in deep water that contains brush or timber. But normally, you just keep moving and searching and trust to luck that you tie into a few.

One exception is on an ice covered lake at the point of an entering stream. Check the temperature of the incoming water. If it is the same as the lake water temperature than forget it. However, if it is about ten or more degrees warmer, you have probably run smack into a bluegill haven. Go to the point where the warmer current descends under the ice. Somewhere around that area there is almost certain to be some nice, big bluegill.

Which baits to use? You can always get an argument among bluegill fishermen as to which is the best bait and winter fishing is no exception. Some swear by the live bait but there is an equal number that wouldn't use anything but an artificial bait and with equal success.

On the live bait side, crickets, earthworms, various larvae, grubs or small strips of pork can be effective. A few fishermen have been known to freeze such tempting bluegill morsels as catalpa worms in the summer, then thaw them out for winter fishing. Another effective bait is the small grub that can be located by cutting open the round blobs found on the stems of goldenrod or horseweeds.

On the artificial side, ice flies, jig-flies or the plastic imitations of live baits such as soft plastic grubs are probably best. You will want to slowly jig the lures at various depths, always keeping them in slow motion. There are times when one pattern or type of lure will turn the bluegill on; other times it will be completely ineffective and you will need to try something else. It is also a pretty well established fact that at times, bluegills will hit the artificial baits rather fiercely and won't touch the live baits. At other times, just the reverse is true.

How to catch them? It requires real fishing finesse to know when to set the hook for winter bluegill. When the line starts to tighten, you need to act rather quickly. If you set the hook too soon or too late, you're going to miss him. You simply have to tangle with a few of them to learn the exact time to set the hook. A very light line in most helpful in letting you know when to strike or set the hook. If you use a bobber, use the smallest one you can find.

To summarize, winter fishing for bluegill can be fruitful. But in all honesty, finding them is usually more luck than skill. On the other hand, how many times have you ever gone fishing when you didn't feel lucky?

CHAPTER 6
HABITAT

The bluegill is so plentiful that few states impose a closed season. It is seldom necessary to make long constly trips for they can practically be found at everyone's door from coast to coast. However, the more you know of their habitat, the more likely it will be that you will consistantly bring home a full stringer of the little scrappers.

The bluegill is predominately a lake fish, preferring the warm, clear water lakes that have an abundance of aquatic vegetation. They will seldon be found in cold, or small, swift flowing streams but will occupy the larger, quiet rivers and streams. This should be your first consideration in looking for bluegill waters.

They normally prefer the weedy areas of lakes rather then brushpiles or stumps. They like to move among the weeds searching for insects and nibbling at the vegetation. The warm, weedy lakes where largemouth bass thrive are usually ideal waters for the bluegill.

They inhabit the water ranging from one foot to twenty feet deep. The depth at which they will be found depends upon time of day, water temperature, season of the year and oxygen content of the water. In the early morning and late evening hours, they move into the shallow, shorelined areas of the lake. In the brighter, mid-hours of the day, they move into the deeper water. If the water becomes very warm or very cold, they normally stay in the deep water.

The water temperature which bluegills prefer will range from 65 to 75 degrees F., with 70 to 72 degrees being most ideal. You should always take the water temperatures into consideration when trying to locate the larger bluegill. The big ones will actually move about the lake searching for water in the neighborhood of 70 degrees.

They like to travel in small schools of usually ten to twenty fish. Unlike crappie, white bass or perch which like to roam all over the lake; the bluegill normally will move back and forth over their home grounds of the shallow, weedy areas where they feed, to their deep water resting places. When you catch a bluegill, it is highly advisable to stay put for there are almost certain to be others nearby. However, it should be noted that bluegill are very sensitive to noise. Any excessive noise will either scare the fish away or make them so wary they won't bite, so it is essential that you be as quite as possible.

The oxygen content of the water is most important as bluegill require more dissolved oxygen than most other fish. This is why bluegill are among the first to die during winter kills of shallow lakes and ponds. Strange as it may seem, in lakes subject to winter kill, you often will find the bluegill fishing better because the population is being held in check.

Unfortunately, the average fisherman has no way to measure oxygen content. However, on hot summer days, if you find that the bluegill has abandoned the deep, cool water, it is probably because of an oxygen shortage at that level and he has moved into an area where it is more plentiful.

CHAPTER 7
FINDING BLUEGILLS

Once we are familiar with the habitat of the bluegill it becomes no great problem to find them if we go about it systematically. This would be true even in new waters of which you are unfamiliar. We will discuss some of the factors that ought to be considered.

First, we would need to consider the season. If it's the spring of the year, we would want to fish the spawning beds as outlined in an earlier chapter. After the spring season, the bluegills move to the deeper water during the day coming into the shallows in early morning, late evening or at night to feed.

One point to remember, when the weather and the water gets hotter as you proceed toward mid-summer, the later the bluegills will feed into the night. Those late summer evenings can be very productive in the shallow coves and along the shore lines. During those summer mid-day hours, the deep water is about your only hope.

You will normally do better if you look for areas that provide cover such as the deep water weed beds. You can often find bluegills around boat houses, rafts, docks or sometimes resting in the shade under an old pier, especially so when the water is deep.

Sometimes, when fishing in very clear water, you can paddle quietly around the lake and spot schools of bluegill, from ten to twenty in a group, just resting near the bottom of the lake. These will normally be found in open patches among the weeds. Two conditions must be met for this method to be successful. One, extremely clear water where you can see the bottom. Second, approach the areas quietly so that you don't spook the fish.

In trying to locate schools of bluegill, it is very important that you fish at various levels. If you are catching only small gills, it probably means that you need to fish deeper for the bigger fish. Once you locate the depth where the big gills are at, you would obviously want to stay at that level.

In the fall, when the water drops to about 70 degrees F., which is the ideal temperature for bluegills, you can find them scattered all over the lake — sometimes shallow, sometimes deep. After the water drops below 70 degrees, your best fishing then is in the shallows that is being warmed by the sun. As the water gets colder, they go deeper, finally settling in the 10 to 20 foot water for the winter.

After the ice thaws out in the spring, the fish scatter. On warm, sunny days, they head for the shallow coves and bays to warm up. On colder days, they stay in the deep. One good spot to look for bluegills during the early, colder part of Spring is around the mouth of streams where the incoming water is warmer than the lake. In fact, bluegill will often swim up these inlet streams to find food and start spawning.

One important point to remember about finding bluegills is that just because you had excellent results in one area during a particular season, does not mean you will have good results in that same area in a different season. In fact, you probably won't due to the seasonal habitat changes of the bluegill. Shallow waters that produced in the spring may be barren by mid-summer. Deep waters that contain bluegill one season may be vacated a couple of months later. However, one rule that normally holds true, and this is a rule that every serious bluegiller should remember--when an area of water at a certain depth produces during a particular month, unless the lake under goes some radical change, that same area at that depth should be a good producer that same month each year.

The reasoning, of course, is quite simple. If the bluegill find an area to their liking during a particular month--proper temperature an oxygen content, etc., in all probability those same conditions will be present during that same month each year.

I am firmly convinced that one of the best assets the serious bluegill fisherman could have is a well documented notebook. I should be filled with information you accumulated on your various fishing excursions. Let's say you went fishing on June 20 and in a particular cove at a depth of 10 feet, you took a full stinger of bull bluegills. You record the date, location, number caught, the hour of day they were biting best and at what depth and any other pertinent information such as water temperature, sunny or over cast sky, etc.

In the following and succeeding years, that information could prove invaluable. On, and around June 20 of each year, you should be able to return to that same cove in happy anticipation of some exciting bluegill action.

CHAPTER 8
NIGHT

The fisherman who has never gone night fishing for blue-gill is overlooking one of the finer aspects of an already fine sport. When the summer sun has been glaring down for weeks in succession, the big bulls will prowl the shoreline during the cool of night looking for insectivorous food. Not only is it pleasant to be on the lake at night but you can have a ball if you luck into a few bluegills along the way.

They can be found along the shoreline shallows as well as the middle of the lake. The big ones will sometimes cruise in schools along the surface. You can locate them by listening for slurping gurgles and a commotion as if they were playing leap frog. Simply move toward the commotion as silently as possible. Small poppers or flies are usually best for this situation. Some fishermen claim that dark colors seem to work best on dark nights, light colors on moonlit nights, however, I don't consider color too important. It's the action of the lure that counts. They seem to hit in a variety of ways and only experience can tell you when to set the hook. Sometimes they will hit the lure fiercely, other times so lightly that you won't know he is there unless you really concentrate on your line every second.

Another method for night fishing is to get a bright lantern, preferable the gasoline or propane type for they are brighter than the older kerosene types. Hang the lantern on your boat and get set for action. The bright lights will attract tiny aquatic organisms which you can see moving about in the water if you look closely. The tiny organisms attract small minnows which in turn attract the bull bluegills. Your best bait for this situation would be small minnows, although you can obtain excellent results with white or yellow jig- flies. Don't be surprised if you take in a few crappie or white bass along with the bluegills.

CHAPTER 9
BULL BLUEGILLS

The runt bluegills usually come easy but hooking those slab-sided bulls requires considerable expertise. No fish is more selective of his table offerings than the large colorful bull. In the early hours of morning he may demand a floating bug, then during the day reject everything except a sinking lure, then from sundown to nightfall, turn his nose up at everything except a tiny gnat. However, to reel in one of those scrappers on ultra light tackle is a thrill of pure enjoyment and one that a person should experience as often as possible.

110

Finding the bull blues can be relaxing as well as rewarding. During the spring spawning season, it is best to start looking along shores that have a gradual slope above water in which the angle of decline continues under the water surface. Start out in 3 to 6 feet of water for you will seldom find the big bulls in shallow water. This is almost worth repeating. Rarely do you find big bulls in shallow water.

During the summer, the 3 to 6 foot depth is still your best bet for taking the bulls in the early and late daylight hours, usually around cover such as weed beds, lily pads, etc. In the heat of day they, of course, have moved into the cooler water in the 10 to 20 foot depth.

The bull bluegills accept both the artificial lures and live bait. When fishing the 10 to 20 foot depth, jig-flies or tiny spoons twitched slowly over bottom cover are usually effective. Small spinners, in the 1/8 ounce range, are good. They should be fished with a slow but steady retrieve just over the bottom. Bulls will also take poppers and a wide assortment of wet and dry flies.

You would normally think that with the bull bluegill being larger, they would wallop the lure with more gusto. Not necessarily so. Sometimes they just inhale the lure and, on occasion, will even move toward you matching the forward motion of your retrieve. Knowing when to set the hook is a skill you must develop. There is just no way to tell you when. You simply develop an instinct for it after enough practice.

I can't verify this but one old timer claims that to catch the biggest of the bulls, he concentrates his efforts during the week following the full moon's peak, just when it's starting to wane.

CHAPTER 10
LIVE BAIT

Bluegills will take a variety of live baits so the fisherman should have an assortment of offerings when he's on the water. The gills can be fussy, especially the jumbos, so the specialist should not fool around when they are biting. Keep switching baits until you find something they want. One day it'll be mealworms, the next day crickets and the next day they may gobble up every red worm in sight and not touch anything else. So keep switching until you find what his diet calls for on a particular day.

The jumbo bluegills are very fond of small minnows. They should be lively minnows, about one inch long. Often you can buy these at a bargain because most fishermen want the larger minnows leaving the bait dealer with a heavy inventory of the smaller ones.

Use a No. 8 hook and put it through the lip or tail of the minnow. Don't put it through the dorsal area as you might do on larger minnows. Because the minnow is small, the spine is so close to the surface of his back that you will probably paralyze the minnow. You want the minnow lively.

In the summer time, the minnows are especially effective when fished early and late in the day around the edges of cover where the water drops to the 10 to 20 foot depths. Set your bobber to where the minnow will be about one foot above the bottom. By staying close to cover, the minnow keeps trying to dart into its shelter and this is what attracts the attention of the jumbo gills.

Running a close second in popularity are tiny, soft crayfish although they are more difficult to find. They should be fished much like the minnow, on a No. 8 hook just off the bottom. Crayfish can also be effective in slow moving streams and also at the point where streams empty into the lake. They also work well in timbered areas around big, dead trees. Usually you can take from one to two large bulls from around each tree. The others will probably be smaller.

The common garden worm has always been a favorite of the bluegill and quite possibly results in the downfall of more bluegills than any other bait. The catalpa worm is also a favorite, especially when inverted. Pinch the head off the worm then place the point of your hook into the worms rear end and skin him onto your hook, wrong side out. This provides a snow-white, juicy offering that is usually tough enough to bring in several bluegills before it is chewed to bits.

During the spring, summer and fall, your most effective live baits would be small minnows, tiny soft crayfish, earthworms, grasshoppers, crickets, catalpa worms and cockroaches. For winter months, only the small baits should be used--mealworms, grubs, larvae, gall worms, maggots, etc.

One point regarding live baits, occasionally the gills will swallow your hook if you fail to set the hook soon enough. And removing a hook from a bluegill can sometimes be a little difficult. One solution is to carry an old washcloth to wrap the fish in as you try to remove the hook. This enables you to easily hold the fish and at the same time protects your hands from the fins. Hold the fish firmly with one hand and grasp the hook with the other. Often times a sharp pointed pair of pliers or a hook disgorger can be very handy tools to have along. Push the barb of the hook through the same hole where it entered the fish. Don't hesitate to use plenty of pressure to do this. It will cause the bluegill less suffering if you get the hook out quickly.

CHAPTER 11
ARTIFICIAL BAITS

Just like the live baits, bluegills will readily take a wide variety of artificial lures. Spinners, poppers, jigs, spiders, flies--you name it (as long as you keep it small) and the bluegill has probably taken it at one time or another.

An excellent way to fish these small lures is to tie them to the end of a 4 lb. monofilament line about 3 feet behind a small plastic bubble or bobber, one that will glide easily over the water without spooking the fish. For a longer cast, you may want to add a small split sinker near the bobber.

The secret to catching fish by this method is in the retrieve. Make a gentle 10 inch pull, then rest 3 seconds to allow the lures to sink deeper, then another gentle 10 inch pull. Continue to do this. Do not wind in steady. Do not make fast jerks.

When fishing lake bottoms in 20 feet of water on hot summer days, or when ice fishing in 20 feet of water in winter, fish them like a jig--a few inches off the bottom with slow up and down movements.

Another excellent method is bottom-bumping. Make a short cast and let your lure sink to the bottom before beginning the retrieve. Then gently lift the lure and reel slowly before bumping bottom again. If the lure doesn't hit bottom solidly when it drops back, set the hook. It usually means that something is on the other end. When you fish this method, be prepared for anything. Most all game fish that swim the bottoms will take small lures when properly presented so be ready for sudden strikes.

One bluegill lure that has gotten a lot of attention in recent years is a green rubber spider. If you are fishing deep, you want the type with sponge bodies that soak up water and sink, not the cellular foam that floats. The most effective type come with white rubber legs.

Success again is in the retrieve. The slower you can move it, the better are your chances.

When the bluegill are surface feeding, they will hit an assortment of gaudy flies and popping bugs. The rubber legs poppers are especially effective but they must be small. When trying to decide which lure to try, these small rubber-leg poppers can be an excellent compromise. They will readily take bluegill, pumpkinseed, rock bass and other bass.

A very slow retrieve is usually most productive with all bugs. I have heard of successful bluegill and bass fishermen who just cast the popper to a likely spot and never even move it. However, most of my success has been from a gentle twitch of the popper every few moments.

During the heat of day bluegill normally refuse all surface baits. Then you must go deep. Very small plugs, tiny spoons or spinners can be effective. Occasionally, the erratic action of a thumb-nail sized spoon will draw a strike while it is still sinking. A small porkrind attached to tiny spoons can also be effective. The lures should always be extremely light. If too heavy,

114

the lure will hit the bottom while the bluegill is still looking around to see what fell in.

Fishing the artificial lures for bluegill can pretty much be summarized in this manner. In the heat of day, the spinning rod with sinking lures is your best bet. In the evening when the gills move into the shallows for surface feeding, the flyrod is probably your best choice.

CHAPTER 12
FLY FISHING FOR BLUEGILLS

Of all methods used for taking bluegills, in all probability, fly-fishing provides the most enjoyable sport. And you will find that on many a day this procedure will bring in your limit. So, let us devote some space to this popular method.

What type of rod to use? This is more of a personal preference. Some fellows prefer an 8 to 8 1/2 foot slow-action rod while others like the lightweight 7 to 7 1/2 footers. A DT-4-F or DT-5-F line is usually most desirably for bluegills to which should be attached an 8 foot, level nylon leader of about a 6 lb. test. The clearer the water, the lighter should be your leader.

What type of flies? Dry flies, wet flies and small bugs are all effective for attacking the bluegill with a fly rod. When one isn't working, sometimes a simple change of pattern or color can start the bluegill to striking.

When it comes to the dry fly patterns, the bluegill usually aren't too particular. Some anglers try to "match the hatch" when possible but this isn't too terribly important. The basic dry fly patterns are all effective and the secret is usually changing colors or patterns until you find one that is working for that particular day.

One of the deadliest surface flies for bluegill (and other sunfish as well) is the foam rubber spider with white rubber legs. Foam rubber is the one that floats. If you want the sinking spider, use the sponge rubber type. It doesn't require much skill to manipulate the rubber spider. Simply cast it and let it float motionless on the water, then occasionally twitch it to make the stretchy legs wiggle. It isn't important that it float high in the water. Often bluegills will hit the spider after it soaks and sinks a few inches. Don't be in too much of a hurry to set the hook. Sometimes the fish can't decide if he wants the spider after swimming several feet toward it. If he bumps the bait set the hook gently. When there aren't any big ones around, the 3-inchers will often tug at the spider legs to keep you interested.

The action of your lure and the method of striking are most important. Have the rod pointed straight at the lure and only occasionally make slight twitches of the line. To set the hook, give the line a short jolt and then bring your rod up only if you feel the fish on. Frequently, the bluegill will nip at the spider several times before taking it. Light strikes with your line only moves the spider a few inches away and it usually teases the bluegill into following to make another pass at it.

For bluegill poppers, any number of finishes are O.K. Red and white, black and white, all black, all white or all yellow are all satisfactory. There are times when the bluegill will prefer one color, at other times another.

When fishing wet flies, you should allow them to sink for several seconds, even two or three minutes at a time if you are wanting to go fairly deep. If your flies aren't sinking deeply enough, you might add a small split shot or even a small spinner. Don't pull or jerk the fly too rapidly for the bluegill won't touch it. Also, if you pull the fly too rapidly, it will not sink enough to attract the larger fish. Be patient for often the bluegill will look at the fly for a long time before moving up and striking.

Which catch the most bluegills, dry or wet flies? Most fishermen agree that most often, the bluegill bite better on wet flies than the dry. However, a good rule of thumb might be--start out with the dry flies. If the fish aren't hitting on the surface, then switch to the sinking flies, going as deep as necessary to start catching the larger fish. Sometimes a difference of only 6 inches of water will mean the difference between strikes and getting skunked. Bluegill can be very selective at times. If you

116

wish, you may use more than one fly by adding dropper loops to your leader.

As I have already mentioned, you can sometimes add a small spinner to your fly and it will be more productive than the fly alone. This is especially so if the water is a bit cloudy or if the fish are deep. Also, a very small piece of pork rind or a small live bait attached to the hook of the fly will sometimes work wonders if the bluegills are reluctant to take the lure into their mouths.

It is of the utmost importance to remember that when fly fishing for bluegill, fish the fly slowly, whether wet or dry. Cast the fly and then let it remain motionless for at least 30 seconds before you even twitch it. Do not drag the fly across the water but rather just barely make the fly flutter and always wait awhile between twitches.

Some of the standard dry fly patterns are: Royal Coachman, Muddler Minnow, Humdinger, Goofus Bug, Hendrickson, Light Cahill, Iron Blue Dun, White Miller, Gray Hackle Red, Grasshopper, Brown Hackle Yellow, Yellow May, Mosquito and others.

Some of the standard wet flies are: McGinty, Western Bee, Black Gnat, Col. Fuller, Professor, Cowdung, Wolly worms (brown, yellow or green). Nymphs (Gray Nymph, Stone Nymph, March Brown Nymph or May Nymph) or sponge-rubber spiders (yellow, black or black and white).

CHAPTER 13
LIGHT TACKLE

On occasion, anglers who own the finest of equipment, have been known to go after bluegill with a cane pole, especially if they're fishing live bait. But this destroys much of the enjoyment for the bluegill is simply no match for the heavier poles. The same could be said for any of the heavier fishing tackle. For maximum fishing enjoyment, ultra-light tackle should be your choice when seeking the bluegill. Also, the lightweights do not tire the user throughout a day of casting.

For the cane pole practitioner, he should consider the fly rod. The fly rod is much more versatile and can even be used to throw natural baits although not by the standard fly casting technique. If you are a live bait enthusiast, be sure to consider the fly rod. Simply fish it like the cane pole and you'll find it provides a much greater thrill when you tie into one of those spunky little fighters. You can also do the same with long, soft spinning rods for they will also cast grubs and worms and do fairly well on small minnows. You should probably avoid the shorter rods for they were intended for snap casts and will often tear the live baits off.

Regardless of whether you fish the surface or the depths, be sure to give the miniature or ultra-light tackle a try. You'll have so much fun that you just might hang up that heavy equipment for good.

CHAPTER 14
WATER TEMPERATURES

Understanding water temperature and how to apply it to the bluegill is one of the best ways to assure yourself of year round fishing success. Remember that bluegills normally stay in water form 1 to 20 feet deep, sometimes deeper. It is the water temperature that normally tells you at what level to start looking for the bluegill. The preferred water temperature for bluegills ranges from 65 to 75 degrees. However, their ideal temperature is 70 to 72 degrees.

In the winter, bluegills go deep to find the most comfortable water possible. Then in the spring, when the water around the edges of the lake warm up to around 67 degrees, they move into the shallow areas to spawn. When summer starts to approach and the shallow waters start to warm they move out into the deeper water, seeking to stay in that 65 to 75 degree level.

Of course, this still leaves you with a lot of water to check out. For summer fishing your ideal situation is to find a spot in the lake where there is some type of cover such as weeds, where the bottom at that point is less than 20 feet, where the water temperature close to the bottom would be 70 to 72 degrees. This would be primarily for mid-day fishing for as we pointed out in an earlier chapter, bluegills move into the shallows for sunrise and twilight feeding.

Don't overlook the temperature factor when searching for bluegill. This one bit of knowledge, when properly applied, can greatly assist you in bringing home those full stringers of bluegill whether it be spring, summer or fall.

CHAPTER 15
FEEDING HABITS

A study in Michigan has found that from May to October, bluegill will consume 336 percent of their body weight but during the other months, will only consume 13 percent of their weight. This tells you at a very fast glance that your best fishing, at least in Michigan, is from May to October. In more southern states, those heavy feeding months would obviously be extended.

The reason for the variation in heavy and light feeding is because food consumption is determined by the metabolism of the bluegill, which depends upon water temperature. If the water temperature is below 55 degrees, the bluegill drastically reduces his food consumption.

During these winter months, the bluegill feed on vegetation, perhaps because the insects have become scarce. They will eat various larvae in the winter, apparently because it offers a change in diet. Since their feeding habits in winter is toward the small larvae, it becomes important that you use very small baits when fishing through the ice or in other cold water.

In the warm months, after a strong wind, look for trees that have toppled into the water. Drop your flies among the branches for the bluegills will swarm into the leafy limbs to search for the hundreds of insects and larvae that thrive in such trees. The action is almost certain to be fast and furious.

Another of the feeding habits of the bluegill that usually has the bluegill expert hopping into his outboard at the first crack of dawn is the mayfly hatch of early summer. Anglers have reported willow trees so loaded with the flies that the twigs bent under their weight. As a breeze or the birds dislodged the flies, there have been reports where the water literally boiled as far as the eye could see as the bluegills gorged on the feast. This scene is often repeated with the emerging of insects as they hatch out and come to the surface of the water. It is when these insects are hatching that you can enjoy some of your finest dry-fly fishing.

Regarding stunted bluegill, there has been an encouraging development that just might solve the problem. It is a known fact that we have millions of acres of inland fresh waters that are already overstocked with fish that have no chance of reaching a decent size because there are just too many fish competing for the available food supply.

According to the Ralston Purina Company, a leading manufacturer of fish foods; bluegill, like most fish and animals, require a balanced ration for optimum growth and this can be achieved by supplemental feeding. Bluegill up to three pounds could easily be obtained with a proper feeding program.

A supplemental feeding program would be ideal for the thousands of small farm ponds across our nation. It could also be practical in large lakes as well. Bluegill establish a home base and will seldom wander more than 60 to 70 yards from that area. By starting a feeding program in a specific area of a lake, one could easily have jumbo bluegills in that particular location.

One of the pioneers in this area was a Mr. Leo Pachner, publisher of Farm Pond Harvest. He not only developed a protein pellet just the right size for bluegill but also perfected a stand-up feeder that could be used in shallow lakes and ponds which holds the pellets at the right location for feeding bluegills.

In one of his studies, he tested 300 stunted bluegills with the protein pellets. In just one season, the growth rate of these fish almost doubled.

Here is the two-fold beauty of such a feeding program, Fat

bluegill, some up to three pounds, will congregate around the feeders by the hundreds providing the fisherman with an absolute blast.

Second, is the proficiency of converting grain into meat. To produce one pound of beef, it requires four pounds of grain. To produce one pound of pork, it requires 3.1 pound of grain. To produce one pound of fish, it requires one pound of grain. Obviously, fish could become our most economical source of edible meat.

If you wish more information about where to obtain the bluegill feeder and the protein pellets, write:

Farm Pond Harvest
372 S. East Avenue
Kankakee, Ill. 60901

CHAPTER 16
SMELLING BLUEGILLS

You no doubt have heard of the bluegill specialists who claim to have been blessed with a beagle nose, so to speak, and can actually smell the schools of bluegills in the water. Some of these old timers claim they can smell the spawning beds. Yet a more recent specialist states that spawning bluegills emit no odor but that they are actually smelling is where a large school of bluegill have simply taken up residence. I personally have never smelled these schools of bluegill, or I have failed to recognize it if I did.

The statement has been made that the odor is extremely delicate and that it dissipates within a few feet of where it rises. They claim that where the odor is found there will always be a conglomeration of debris or thick vegetation covering the bottom at that point. They further claim that the uninformed often times mistake the bluegill odor for the odor of perfumed blossoms.

In trying to describe the odor, one specialist claims the only thing he knows of that has a similar odor is oil of anise. If you wish to check it out, buy a vial of anise oil from your druggist, place a few drops on a cloth, then hold the cloth over your nose. and breath slowly for several minutes. Then when you are on the water and you detect that odor, you are supposed to be directly over a thriving school of bluegills. However, if you fail to locate any bluegill by this method, please don't hold me responsible. I haven't actually said that I believe in it.

CHAPTER 17
DESCRIPTION

The bluegill belongs to the sunfish family Centrarchudae. This family also includes the largemouth and smallmouth black bass, crappie, rock bass, warmouth bass and various species of the true sunfish such as redear, pumpkinseed, yellowbreast, spotted, etc. The bluegill is similar in appearance to the other true sunfish but it does have some different features.

The color of the bluegill varies but normally it is a dark olive-green on the back with a purple like cast on the sides. The breast of the male is yellow to bright red while the female is white to pale yellow.

In clear water, the colors are generally brighter, in muddy water they are usually more pale. Most sunfish have bright-colored spots on their sides but these are absent on the bluegill. Instead there is usually from 6 to 8 dark- colored vertical bars on each side of the bluegill. You will also find a dark blotch on the end part of the dorsal fin near the body of the fish. The dorsal fin is a single fin with ten spines. The pictoral fins are pointed and rather long. The tail is not sharply forked as some other species and its tail tips are rounded. On the border of the opercle flap you will find no trace of a red spot as you will on many of the other sunfish.

When bluegill are first hatched, they usually run from 2 to 3 millimeters in length. Conditions of the water effect their growth rates. In heavily populated waters of low fertility they are sometimes so stunted, they never grow longer than 6 inches regardless of age. But in the high fertility waters, such as the warm waters of the south with its longer feeding periods, then they will frequently exceed 10 inches in length and over a pound in weight. However, this exceeds their average size. In a study made from various states of the average growth of bluegills, the following represents the national average:

End of Year	Length of growth in inches
1st Year	1.9
2nd Year	3.7
3rd Year	5.3
4th Year	6.0
5th Year	6.8
6th Year	7.7

The death rate of bluegills is high. This is true for most fish. One study has indicated that if you start out in a fishing season with 100 bluegills; 24 will be caught, 44 will die sometime during the year and 32 will survive until the next season. You can quickly see that out of the 100 fish, only 1 in 5 is caught by the fisherman. It is obvious that fishing has little effect on the total population of the bluegill. It has been proven on many occasions that there is no reason to limit the season nor size or number of bluegill caught. It is worth repeating that all bluegill caught, regardless of size, should be kept. Happily, you should be encouraged to catch as many as possible, as often as possible.

The majority of bluegill fail to live more than 5 years. In a study of 5,464 bluegill, it was found that 91% was less than 4 years of age. Only 8% had reached the 5 year mark.

Since the bluegills live such a short life span, it is obvious that for them to achieve maximum growth, they should have adequate food available from the start of their life span.

CHAPTER 18
FREEZING THE BLUEGILL

One of the misconceptions about freezing bluegill (and most other fish) is that they need to be cleaned before you toss them into the freezer. Most experts now agree that it just isn't so.

Here's a little experiment you might try just to satisfy yourself. On your next mess of bluegill, take a few of the fish, cut off their heads, gut them, scale them, wash each piece then carefully wrap and put them in the freezer.

Take the rest of the fish and toss them in a bag as is (no dressing or cleaning) and put them in the freezer with the other fish.

Six months later, take out both packages of fish and thaw them out. Immediately clean and dress the fish that were put in whole, then cook both packages of fish at the same time, being careful to keep them separate so you know which is which.

You will be pleasantly surprised to find that the fish you had frozen whole will be firm and fresh as the day you caught them while the ones you had cleaned prior to freezing will probably be somewhat mushy and have a tendency to fall apart.

The old theory that if you don't take out the guts and gills, the fish will spoil is simply not supported by the evidence. It has been suggested that perhaps by freezing the slime around the fish, it apparently helps to retain the fish's freshness.

In fact, here's even a better way. Take a mess of freshly caught bluegill and toss them whole into a plastic bag (no cleaning, dressing, or washing). Fill the bad with water, then place the plastic bag of water and fish in the freezer and freeze it into a ball of ice. The evidence seems to suggest they will keep indefinitely in this manner.

CHAPTER 19
CLEANING BLUEGILLS

You have just arrived home from a successful excursion on the nearby lake and the stringer is full of fat little bluegills. You may wish to pop them into the freezer as described in the last chapter. If so, you should do so immediately to preserve their freshness and flavor.

However, you may wish to indulge in some fine eating that same day. If so, the bluegills should be cleaned quickly. Every hour you wait detracts from their optimum flavor.

There are various methods for cleaning bluegill but the one we are describing here we think is the easiest and quickest. Before starting, you should assemble all the proper tools such as a large board, scale remover, sharp knife and a pair of lightweight cotton gloves. Then call your wife in and tell her to get with it.

If this doesn't work, and for most of us husky men it usually doesn't, here's the next best procedure.

First, the fish should be scaled. Next, turn the fish belly-side up and make a "V" cut to remove anus. At the same time, disconnect the intestines at that point. Then lay the fish on his side and just behind the gill flaps cut through the spine, severing the upper part of the head from the body. Leave the lower part of the head attached. Now get a firm hold onto the body, push on the head with a knife and as the head comes off the innards will stay with the head. Then remove the dorsal fin, finish cutting off any remains of the lower head and what you have left is good meat with little bone. They should then be washed and soaked in salt water for an hour or so before cooking.

CHAPTER 20
COOKING THE BLUEGILL

Probably the most popular method for cooking bluegill is to first dip them in buttermilk, then shake them in a bag of salted flour, then deep fry until a golden brown. It is extremely simple and easy to do and all the fancy recipes in the world won't improve on this method.

Another method is to simply roll in cornmeal and quick fry in hot grease. Doesn't make much difference. You can't go wrong either way.

For a little variety, you might try one or two of the following.

Bluegills In Beer

Take one cup pancake mix, one egg, one teaspoon salt and one cup of beer. Mix these ingredients together to form a batter. Dip your bluegill fillets in the batter, then lower them one at a time into a preheated cooking oil of 360 degrees. Cook approximately two minutes or until golden brown. Drain and serve.

Baked Bluegill

Take six whole dressed bluegills (no fillets), one cup of milk, one teaspoon of salt, twelve thin bacon strips, blanched, two tablespoons butter plus one- third cup of melted butter and lemon wedges.

Put the teaspoon of salt into the milk and soak the bluegills in this for twenty minutes. Now wrap two slices of bacon around each bluegill and place them in a bake dish that was buttered with the two tablespoons of butter. Bake for twenty minutes, uncovered, in a preheated 400 degrees oven, basting frequently with the melted butter. Serve with the lemon wedges.

Bluegill Stuffing

Have you ever had a batch of small bluegill that seemed too small to bother with but you hated to throw them away? Well, here's what you can do. Make them into a stuffing. Who said stuffing had to be made out of bread anyway?

Let's assume you have a nice five pound bass or some other large fish and several small bluegill. To start with, you have to get the bluegill flesh off the bone. Try partially cooking the bluegills in simmering water. Just as they are starting to cook, take them out, skin them and then pull the meat off the bones. You will want about one pound of bluegill flesh picked free of bones, then chopped fine or you could run it through a grinder.

Now melt two tablespoons of butter and blend in two tablespoons of flour. Cook this mixture for one minute, then remove it from the heat. Stir in one cup of hot milk with a slice of onion, a sprig of parsley and a bay leaf in it. Now heat this mixture to a boil, then add the chopped bluegill and stir well.

Now add two eggs, one at a time, and beat well. Season with salt and pepper and a dash of nutmeg. You now have enough stuffing to stuff a four or five pound fish.

TRICKS THAT
TAKE CATFISH

CHAPTER 1
THE CATFISH

There's an old saying that a man has to be crazy to be a catfish fisherman. This, of course, is not true. But it helps.

There are days when a nice frozen shrimp or a neat grass-hopper will bring in a fine string of catfish. Other days they won't draw a single nibble but the fellow fishing next to you, using some thoroughly ripened chicken entrails, will be hauling them in as fast as he can throw out his line. That's catfishing.

There have probably been more wild tales inspired by the catfish than any other species. Like the time they caught a catfish in Arkansas that was so big when they pulled it out, the water level of the lake dropped two feet. Or, the time in Texas when two fellows hooked a catfish on a rope that was attached to their jeep. With that 4-wheel drive jeep pulling one way and the catfish pulling another, something had to give. They lost the catfish but claim to hold the world record for pulling out a 65 pound lower jaw bone.

To set the record straight, there are over 1000 species of catfish around the world. They range in size from tiny tots no bigger than a match head to monsters weighing a few hundred pounds.

In the United States, the most popular native species are the black bullhead, brown bullhead, yellow bullhead, white catfish, blue catfish, channel catfish and the flathead catfish.

All of these fellows have several things in common. Each has eight whiskers which are called barbels. One long pair trails from each corner of the mouth, two more rise near the nostrils and four more project from under the chin.

The incredible aspect of these whiskers, or barbels, is that they are covered with extremely sensitive taste buds which enables a catfish to zero in on his food long before he can even see it. He can actually taste his food without even opening his mouth. It is for this reason that catfish can easily be caught in muddy water.

Unlike most fish, catfish have no scales. However, they are not without their protection for they possess three sharp, stiff spines which are capable of inflicting rather painful wounds, the two pectorals and the dorsal.

The pectorals, which are the two forward fins, have poison glands at their base. Should you ever be "horned" by the catfish, the poison will enter your bloodstream as the spine enters your skin. It is not a deadly poison but can become quite painful if not given prompt first aid.

One of the better antidotes for the pain and infection is bacitracin, which can be obtained at your local druggist. Simply dab it on the wound and cover with a band-aid.

Although it has this menacing feature, it is almost impossible to look a catfish in the face and not feel sorry of it. When it came to handing out good looks, Mother Nature really short-changed the catfish for it is, without much question, one of the world's ugliest fish.

He has probably been cussed and discussed and praised and damned more than any other fish in the United States. However its ugliness is only skin deep for beneath the slippery hide is some eating of the highest quality. There are many connoisseurs of fresh waterfish who claim the catfish is the best tasting of all.

Which brings us to the various and sundry ways of taking catfish. There are so many ways for putting catfish on the string that it is almost certain you will find one or two of the methods to your liking. They can be taken on rod and reel, throw line, set lines, trot lines, jug lines and other methods. We will discuss all of these in later chapters. Some of these methods are illegal in some states. Be sure you are aware of what you can and cannot do legally in your particular state.

When and where to go catfishing? The best time to go is always whenever you can get away. However, the optimum months for the best catches are usually the early summer months of April, May and June and the fall months of September and October, depending on which part of the country you live in.

All catfish have eight whiskers (or barbels) that are covered with extremely sensitive taste buds. They enable a catfish to zero in on his food long before he can even see it. This is the reason catfish can easily be caught in muddy water.

If everything were equal (it usually isn't when it comes to fishing) the person who would catch the most catfish would be the person who kept his baited hook in the water the longest. The law of averages would see to that.

However, this is usually not true because things usually are not equal. There are certain long practiced proven techniques for taking catfish consistently. The person who masters these techniques is almost certain to bring home much larger catches much more often than the person who goes about it haphazardly. The purpose of this book is to acquaint you with, and enable you to master, those proven techniques.

CHAPTER 2
HABITAT

In later chapters we will explore the various methods for taking catfish but before we do, it is essential that we learn something of the catfish's habitat if we want to make consistently large catches. It would do little or no good to be fishing in one part of the lake if the catfish were mostly in some other area. Your chances for success will be greatly increased if we know where the catfish are most likely to be and when they are most likely to be feeding.

Catfish of one species or another is found in at least forty-six of our fifty states. They are mostly all bottom dwellers, cruising along the bottoms of lakes, rivers and ponds. Although they have very small eyes, they are almost blind. However, this is offset be an extremely keen sense of smell and touch. Their barbels become their feelers and since they particularly feed by smell, the stink baits of various kinds are quite successful.

All catfish are mostly nocturnal feeders which is another way of saying they feed mostly at night. They will often bite during the day but your chances for fast action are far better late in the evening and at night, usually from dusk until about midnight.

Catfish, like most other fish, want to be comfortable. They seek an area where the water temperature is to their liking.

This is one of the first requirements to become successful at catfishing is to know their preferred water temperatures and where they are most likely to be at during a given time of the day or night of a particular season.

WINTER HABITAT

In the winter, catfish go deep and become quite inactive. Although catfish can be caught the year round in our southern states, it is extremely rare that you will catch one during the winter in our northern states. If you live in the northern states, it is usually best that once the water starts to really get cold, to forget about catfish until the following spring. It has been reported that ice fishermen have seen catfish swimming about under the ice but could seldom catch one. They just refuse to feed when the water gets too cold.

However, in the southern states catfishing can be quite profitable. It seems that the catfish have a way of holing up for the winter. If you can find one of those winter holes, you stand an excellent chance of bringing in several nice ones. Stink baits seem to be the favorite of southern fishermen, the kind they stir up out in the shed away from the house. If you don't have the stomach for this kind of bait, the "store bought" baits can also be very effective for winter fishing in our southern waters.

SPRING HABITAT

It is after the winter season is over that you enter the best season for taking catfish. When the water temperature warms up to over 50 degrees, you can start to have fair success. However, it is after the water temperature goes over 60 degrees that you will have your fastest action.

It is always best to go by water temperatures rather than the calendar. Some years you will have an early or later season depending on how fast the waters warm up. This is certainly true in comparing some sections of the country to others. Your timing will be far better if you stay abreast of the temperatures and let this be your guide rather than the seasons.

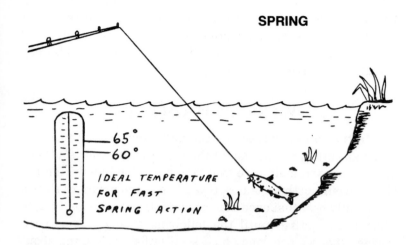

In the spring, catfish began to forage for food in earnest to make up for the weight and strength they lost during the winter. You will have fair success when the waters go over 50 degrees but the action gets much faster after the waters go over 60 degrees.

It is during the spring that catfish begin to forage for food in earnest to make up for the weight and strength they have lost during the winter. During the hours of darkness, they like to move into the shallows and feed and then return to their favorite holes during the day. If it is a spring overcast, cloudy or drizzly day, they will often remain in the shallows and continue feeding until the condition changes. This is an excellent time to be on the water if you want fast action.

Most authorities agree that the most productive time of the year for taking catfish is in the late spring of the year when the water temperature is between 60 to 65 degrees. They can be taken during the daylight hours but again the authorities agree that the best time is just before dark until about midnight.

SPAWNING SEASON

Once the water reaches temperatures between 65 to 75 degrees, the catfish disperse over large areas and begin to spawn. Unlike many other species, such as bluegill or crappie, where the fishing is usually at its peak during the spawning season, the catfish hardly feeds while they are spawning. You may catch one occasionally, but they will come far and inbetween.

When they start to spawn, they will look for a natural nest such as a cavity or impression in the mud. Nests have been found in such places as cattle tracks in the mud, under submerged logs, under old stumps, in old rusty buckets, in old field tiles, in hollow logs, under the roots of cattails and in tin cans.

If no natural nest is available, the male and female will work together preparing a nest by using their pectoral spines as picks and their mouths as shovels. The female then lays her eggs, usually from 2,000 to 6,000, which she deposits in a gelatinous mass. This will usually be in water from 6 inches to 4 feet deep.

For a while, both the female and male will guard the nest. After a period of time, the female either leaves or is driven away by the male. The male then continues to guard the nest and keep the eggs clean. He does this by working his fins and tail over the eggs and will occasionally take them in his mouth and works them around as you would a mouthwash, then puts them back in his nest.

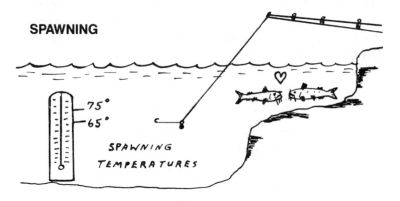

SPAWNING

Catfish spawn when water temperatures are between 65 to 75 degrees. Unlike crappie and bluegill, catfish feed very little during spawning season.

The water temperature determines the incubation period with the average running from three to five days.

After the eggs hatch, the male continues to guard the school of fish, keeping them together in the shallows and out of danger until they are almost two inches in length.

If danger occurs, he will stir up the mud, creating a mud screen to provide a getaway route for the small ones. Protective though he may be, he will occasionally forget his fatherly duties and gobble up one of the young ones he is suppose to be guarding from harm. The ones that survive his loving care will usually stay together in the shallow water seeking protection among the aquatic vegetation.

SUMMER AND FALL HABITAT

After spawning season is over, catfish spread out. They are not a schooling fish such as bass, crappie or bluegills but usually move about as a solitary cruiser constantly searching for food. They will normally stay in the deeper, more comfortable water during the day and move into the shallows to start feeding just before dark.

Catfish are a natural stream fish, although they are quite adaptable to ponds, lakes and man-made impoundments. In large bodies of water, they will often gather where creeks or rivers empty into the reservoir because they provide the current which catfish like for feeding as well as reproducing. In rivers, they are seldom found in the stream's current but rather will pick a quieter eddy water near the current. This way they are close enough to spot anything eatable that might be washed downstream without having to fight the moving water.

Catfish seem to be as much at home in sluggish, murky streams as they are in the fast moving, clear waters. The bull-head is more likely to be found in muddy waters than he is in clean water. This is where he gets the nickname of "mud cat".

Channel cats are somewhat different. They prefer the swifter currents of cleaner streams or the clean stretches of bottom in deep, clear lakes.

CHAPTER 3
WATER CONDITIONS

Changing water conditions probably affect the catfish more than any other fish. After a heavy rain when waters start to rise, catfish go on a feeding spree. The same is true while the water is receding. But as soon as the water returns to normal, the action dramatically slacks off.

So, the next time you have a heavy rain and the waters start to rise, get moving. You won't find a better time for taking cats.

As a matter of fact, if you happen to have access to waters below a reservoir, you needn't wait for it to rain. When the gates of the various dams are opened to release the surplus water, you have the same situation. As the rushing water loosens debris along the way, the hungry catfish commence stuffing their bellies.

The same is true in reservoirs that are located below other man-made impoundments. When the overflow water from one reservoir flows down stream and then into another one to make a quick change in the water level, the catfish start feeding like crazy.

Sometimes you can run into some wild fishing when a stream has overflowed its normal bed. Catfish will move into grassy areas exploring the new feeding area. When conditions are right, you will catch them almost as fast as you can throw out your bait.

Although rising waters affect all catfish, it probably turns the channel cat on most of all. The channel cat loves a current and it will often move right into the swift water to feed. However, the real hot spots for channel cats are the back eddies where the current swirls and agitates food.

When waters are on the rise or at flood stage, the waters will be somewhat muddy. It is during this period that cats feed primarily by smell. Your stink baits or strong smelling baits are your best bet under these conditions. There have been reports of

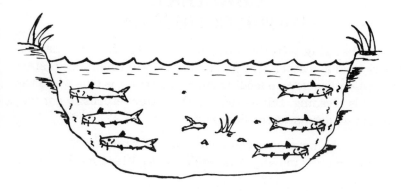

After a heavy rain when streams start to rise and the rushing water loosens debris along the way, catfish go on a feeding spree. They also go on a feeding spree when the waters start to recede.

good results with frozen shrimp. The shrimp has a distinctive odor and since it is white, can be seen fairly easily even in murky water.

There is not much question that sometimes a one day wait can be the difference between success and failure. If the waters have been normal for awhile and suddenly start to rise, you may notice that a few of your fellow employees didn't show up for work. You can be reasonably assured that you have some knowledgeable catfish fishermen around.

CHAPTER 4
FEEDING HABITS

As we have previously mentioned, catfish are primarily nocturnal foragers. It doesn't make much difference which season of the year you are fishing for them, the best time of day is just before dark until about midnight. When the sun touches the horizon and darkness starts to fall, Mr. Catfish comes out of hiding and starts on a feeding spree. So, if we are to match wits with the catfish, it will be well to remember this one aspect of his feeding habits.

Although cats are primarily bottom feeders, there are occasions when they can be taken fairly successfully just below the surface. This can be true after a rise in the water. As the water starts to settling back to normal but is still slightly off-color, catfish can be taken on bobber with the hook and sinker about two feet below the bobber. What has happened is that the high waters have washed insects and worms from the banks and the catfish are moving about enjoying the feast. Most of these tidbits are being carried near the surface by the current instead of being allowed to concentrate near the bottom.

Catfish are omnivorous feeders and will eat many kinds of plant, animal and insect material. Their natural diet consists of such items as algae, plant remains, fish, frogs, microscopic crustaceans, nymphs, pond weeds of various kinds, seeds from water lilies and other plants, fish remains, mollusks (clams and snails) crawfish, aquatic insect larvae, adult insects and other items such as fish eggs, etc.

We have already mentioned that catfish spend most of their time on the bottom. A great deal of this time is spent just moving along the bottom looking for something to eat. This should always be remembered as a basic characteristic of their feeding habits. You will normally have your best success with catfish when you fish right on or off the bottom.

Here are a couple of pointers for some fast catfish action. If you have access to some of the big dams in our country, the fishing below those dams can be fabulous. Here's why. The big turbines used for generating electricity are constantly drawing in bait fish and grinding them into little pieces. The blood and odor from those chopped-up fish draw the catfish by the hundreds. If you want to go after one of the big babies -- in the 50 to 60 pound range, this is an excellent place to start.

A word of caution is in order. The turbulent water below those dams can be treacherous so use every precaution. We have a dam across the Ohio River close to Cincinnati that has claimed more than one life. This particular dam has an overflow at the top as most river dams do. As the water plunges over the dam into the lower water, it creates a back current. Boats that get too close are drawn into the overflow and capsized. As long as you stay back from the overflow, it is no more dangerous than any other part of the river.

In the event you don't live near such a dam, here is a little trick you can try that will get about the same results.

Pick out an area you like to fish and for a period of several days throw in some pieces of decayed meat, fish or corn meal. The catfish will start to congregate around the area and you can then go out with your rod and reel and have a ball.

Catfish are primarily bottom feeders. You will normally have your best success by keeping your baits right on or very near the bottom.

CHAPTER 5
TACKLE

Down through the years, one of the basic tools for bringing in cats was the old cane pole. However, anyone who has ever caught a catfish or any other kind of a fish on light tackle, would never go back to the cane pole. Hoisting a catfish out with a long, stiff bamboo pole simply doesn't provide the enjoyment that a light-weight rod and reel will. Not only that, with a bamboo pole, you are very limited in the range you can cover whereas with the rod and reel you can greatly expand this area.

My personal choice for tackle is the same light tackle I would use for most other panfish. I am thinking primarily of taking cats in the 2 to 6 pound range. This tackle will provide you with far greater sport and also will produce more fish. I will normally use a 10 lb. test monofilament line with a No. 4 hook. If you are using a bobber, it should be adjusted so the bait is only 2 or 3 inches off the bottom.

A very excellent rig for catfish is to use a dipsey sinker tied to the very end with one or two dropper loops about a foot or two up from the sinker. This type rig allows for easy casting and puts one of the baits right at the bottom with other baits for different levels. If you are fishing from shore, this rig is a fine choice because you can cast it a long distance.

Of course, if you are going for the larger size cats, you would probably want a 20 pound test line with possibly a size 1/0 or 2/0 hook. And, if you are out for the monsters, your line should be in the 40 to 100 pound test range with a corresponding size hook as well as a much heavier rod and reel.

If the water current is pretty strong, you may need to add a heavier sinker to get the bait down on the bottom. This is essential for as we have already noted, cats are primarily bottom feeders.

When casting with bait, you want to avoid the snap cast. It is better if the bait is more or less lobbed out. Any sudden jerk might cause the bait or a heavy sinker to break off.

Heavy sinkers do have one disadvantage for they can prevent a person from detecting a bite. One rig that helps to avoid this is to put a light-weight pinch-on sinker about one foot ahead of the hook. Above this, have a heavy slip-sinker. The heavy slip-sinker will carry the bait to the bottom and hold it stationery in the current, the pinch sinker will prevent the slip sinker from jamming against the bait.

The advantage to this type rig is that it offers a more direct link between fish and the angler and the fisherman can easily detect a bite. Quite often, a catfish will pick up a bait and then drop it so unless you detect the bite and strike quickly you might miss him.

If you are using worm globs, dead bait or stink baits, it is usually not necessary to give him much slack before you sock it to him. However, on live baits, it is normally better to let him run ten to twelve feet before you strike. By this time he should have turned the bait and at least partially swallowed it.

Another advantage to using a rod and reel is that you can move about until you locate fish. You should usually not stay at one spot for more than 30 minutes without a bite. When catfish are feeding, they will normally go to it in a hurry.

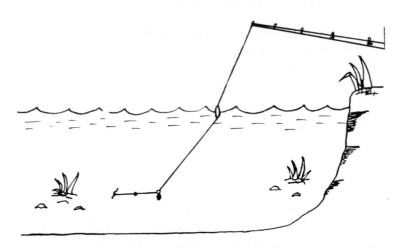

When fishing in a current, you need a heavy sinker to get the bait to the bottom. A slip sinker should be used as it will do the job, yet still allow you to detect a bite. A pinch-on sinker one foot above the hook prevents the slip sinker from sliding against the bait.

Still another advantage to the rod and reel is that you can use artificial baits for the channel catfish. This fellow will hit plugs, jigs, flies, pork- rind baits, etc. He is an easy fellow to please.

CHAPTER 6
TROTLINES

One of the more enjoyable ways for taking catfish and certainly one of the most productive is by trotlines. I still recall as a youngster in Kentucky the nights we spent on the banks of the Licking River and Slate Creek. We would run the trot lines every two hours and I'll never forget the thrill of starting to pull the line and feel the tug of a big cat thrashing to get off. It is one of my more enjoyable childhood memories.

The first step to taking fish by trotline is to check your respective state laws. Be sure you know what you can and cannot do legally. The trotline is illegal in some states. In other states there is a limit on the number of hooks you can use. In some states live rough fish such as carp can't be used for bait.

Once you get past this point, the rest should be easy. Catfish can be caught on trot lines in creeks, rivers, lakes, farm ponds or man-made impounds.

One of the secrets for successful trotline fishing is to select a good location. Sometimes, moving your line a few hundred yards up or down stream can be the difference in a full or empty string. I recall on one occasion that we set two lines across a long pool in the Licking River. One line was set near the center where it was fairly deep. The other was about fifty yards upstream at the shallow end of the pool. We didn't catch a single fish on the one at the center of the pool but caught several nice cats on the one at the shallow end. So, if you are not having any luck at one spot, move to another location.

If you plan to try trot-lining, one of your most important considerations is to have a properly constructed rig. In case you are not familiar, trot-lining is nothing more than anchoring a strong main line across a river or narrow inlet of a lake, quite frequently by tying it to low lying tree limbs on each side. They can also be set out in a lake by tying each end to a water buoy such as plastic gallon jugs and anchor the jugs with heavy weights.

The main line should be as long as needed with a normal trotline running from 30 to 100 feet. These main lines should be of a heavy material of considerable strength, usually of white cotton or braided nylon. To this main line are attached many short lines with hooks. These short lines are called "stagings" or "drop lines". They are normally from 15 to 25 inches long and are usually spaced about 3 feet apart on the main line.

The size hook you use is up to the individual fisherman. If you are out for the big fellows, you might want a size No. 5/0. You, of course, should realize that a hook of this size will prevent many smaller size cats from getting hooked. A seize No. 3/0 is usually sufficient for most catfish.

The choice of bait is again up to the fisherman. There must be a hundred different baits you can choose from such as liver, small fish, cut up pieces of fish, etc. We'll devote a whole chapter to this later. My personal choice is to use an assortment of different baits since you may have up to 30 hooks in the water. This way a cat can turn his nose up at one of the offerings but find another to his liking.

Trotlines can be quite elaborate such as having swivels and clamps to keep the stagings from slipping on the main line. Or, they can be plain as mud with the stagings tied directly to the main line. In my younger days, we tied them directly to the main line and then rolled it into a big ball. I can tell you it was quite a job trying to unroll that ball. Those many hooks could really jam it up.

I haven't set a trotline since I was a teenager but if I should do so again, I would rig it like this.

I would have the main line of nylon as this will last indefinitely in or out of water. I would want one in the range of 100 pound test or more. If you ever get 2 or 3 big cats on there at the same time you'll need a strong line. About every 3 feet along the line, I would attach a small metal ring.

The drop line would be a 20 or 30 pound test line about 18 inches long. At one end would be a size No. 3/0 or 4/0 hook. At the other end would be a small metal snap--the type you buy at the hardwood store, the kind you usually find at the end of a dog leash. About midway between the hook and snap, I would insert a high quality barrel swivel. This will prevent your line from twisting as the fish fights for freedom.

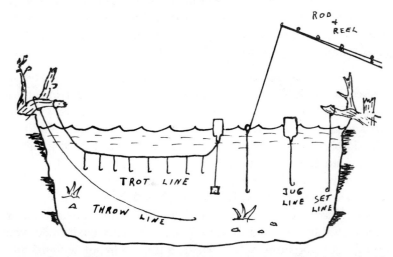

There are so many ways for putting catfish on the string that it is almost certain every fisherman should find one or two methods to his liking.

With a rig of this type, the main line could be rolled into a neat ball and the drop lines stacked neatly in a box until needed. As you move your boat along the main line, you simply bait a hook, snap the drop line onto the metal ring and you are in business.

I'm not sure if there is such a thing as a correct way to string a trot line. Some fishermen put weights on the line to keep the hooks near the bottom. Others attach floats to the line to keep it suspended in the water. As a youngster, I don't recall doing either of these things. We just stretched them across the river. And we caught a lot of catfish.

If you have never seem a trot line, possibly you are still confused as to how they should be rigged. Perhaps you are experiencing a problem I experience each spring. I read the simple instructions our government puts out each year on how to fill out my income tax form and they have never failed to confuse me yet.

If such is the case, you would probably be better off to buy a commercial trot line. A good one can be bought for about $5.00. After you see how easily they are put together, you will more likely want to rig your own after that.

Where you set the trot line is pretty much a matter of choice. If the line is long enough, you may want to go from shore to shore. If the river is too wide, or if you are on a lake; you can anchor one end to a tree limb on shore, and the other end to a plastic bottle such as a Clorox jug. You would need a heavy weight anchored to the jug to keep it stationery. Or, if you wished, you could run the line parallel to shore. This can often be an excellent position for as we previously mentioned, when the sun starts to set, the cats begin to move from the deep water to the shallows to feed. If your line is properly positioned, you should get some fine action. Deep, quiet pools below dams and riffles are often productive spots. Another good spot is where a creek or river empties into a lake.

It is pretty much agreed that the best time to set a trot line is just when it is starting to get dark. Once you have the line set and baited, you should check it about every two hours to hold any losses to a minimum. You should do this throughout the night, or until you get so sleepy that it doesn't seem worth while.

A must piece of equipment is a good sized, sturdy landing net. Frequently, a big cat will not be hooked well enough that you can lift him out of the waters and it can result in the loss of your best catch of the night. Slip the net under him while he is still in the water. It's good insurance.

CHAPTER 7
SET LINES

This form of fishing for catfish has developed a number of titles. In various parts of the country they refer to it as set lines, set poles, bank lining, bankpoling, set-hook fishing, etc. Basically, they are all the same. It involves tying a drop line to an overhanging branch or a pole that had been forced into the river bank. It is very similar to trot line fishing but instead of attaching the drop lines to a main trot line, you attach the drop lines to tree limbs.

It is not a new form of fishing and it is rather surprising that more fishermen do not employ this method. If you are interested in fishing for meat, this is an excellent way to put it on the table. As in the case of the trot lines, you should check your state laws as set lining is illegal in some states.

Set lines can be set along any creek, river or lake bank. The line can be from 3 or 4 feet long to 8 or 10 feet, depending on the water depth and how deep you want to fish. You should use the same type of hook and bait you would use on the trot line. You may fish it right on the bottom if you wish or at any level you prefer. A heavy sinker is normally used to keep the bait either on or close to the bottom.

One of the advantages of tying the set line to a limb is that it has spring. If a catfish becomes hooked, he cannot get a strong pull against the line to break it. Also, it tends to wear him down until the fisherman comes along to pull him in.

You may set 3 or 4 lines along the bank or 3 or 4 dozen, depending on how ambitious you are. The lines should be checked about every two hours just as you would a trotline. Of course they should be re-baited if a fish has cleaned the hook.

They should be set during the evening at about the same time you would set a trot line. Your main problem is to remember where you tie each line so they can be easily located. There is always an element of suspense as you approach each line and needless to say, it's always a thrill when the limb is springing up and down with a big cat on the other end of the line.

CHAPTER 8
THROW LINE

Throw line fishing is quite similar to set line fishing. The only real difference is in the length of the line. In set line fishing, the line is rather short and hangs straight down from a tree limb or set pole with the bait just a few inches off the bottom.

In throw line fishing, the line can be as long as you want. You simply tie the line to some object on the bank, bait the hook and throw it out to settle on the bottom until a wandering catfish comes along. The line could be 10 to 12 feet long or 40 to 50 feet long if you wish.

Of the various methods we have discussed, this is probably the least productive. Unless the catfish swallows the baits, he stands a good chance of not getting hooked. This is because there is no resistance at the other end of the line, since the line is laying limp across the bottom. (With the trot line, set line and jug fishing, there is resistance due to the tension of the main line, the limb or the jug. This resistance not only helps hook the fish but plays a major role in keeping him hooked.)

The exception for throw-line fishing is when you are watching the line and you set the hook if you get a bite. A relaxing way to do this is to tie the line around your leg and then take a nap. However, this method should be avoided by youngsters and lightweight persons. They might get pulled into the water. Throw line fishing is almost the same as "dead line" fishing with a rod and reel. This is where you cast out your bait and let it settle to the bottom (no bobber). The only difference at all is that a throw line can be left all night and then checked the next morning, whereas the rod and reel is usually held in hand waiting for a tug on the other end of the line.

I have a son that strives for the better part of two worlds. He loves to fish with a jig-fly for crappie, bluegill and anything else that will hit. He's also a devoted fan of the channel cat. I've seen him take two and sometimes three fishing rods on a trip. His first move is to load up his heavy tackle with a gob of night crawlers, toss them out deadline, set the lock on his reels and then lay them down. Now he takes his light fishing rod and starts casting around fallen trees and other objects for crappie or bluegill while he waits for a channel cat to come along. He usually comes home with a few of all three.

CHAPTER 9
JUG FISHING

Jug fishing employs the same principal as both the trot line and the set line and yet it is different for it has some distinct advantages over the other methods. When you set a trot line or set pole, they remain stationary and unless the catfish moves into the area where the bait is at, it's obvious you won't catch him. The big advantage with jug fishing is that it takes the bait to the catfish. It is especially effective for once a catfish gets hooked, he soon wears himself out tugging at the jug and the tension against the jug helps to keep him on the hook.

All you need for this type of fishing is a plastic bottle such as a Clorox bottle or any type of an air-tight container that will float. Although I've never tried it, there's no reason that a big

JUG FISHING

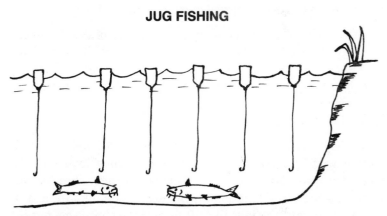

Jug fishing is a fairly new method for taking catfish. It has one advantage over trot lines and set lines in that as the jugs move with the wind or current, they carry the bait to the catfish. In big areas, a floating jug will often expose the bait to a large number of catfish.

piece of styrofoam or even a chunk of wood wouldn't serve the same purpose as long as it floats.

You simply tie a drop line to the floating jug with a baited hook on the other end and toss it in the water and let it float. When the jug starts to bob up and down, you merely retrieve it and remove the fish.

The hook size should be determined by the fisherman, depending on what size fish he is after. Same is true for the strength of the line.

The length of the line should be determined by a number of factors. If you are fishing at night, you would probably not want the lines over 3 or 4 feet in length. We have mentioned that catfish move into the shallows at night to feed. Obviously, we will want a fairly short line that will keep the bait near the bottom in shallow coves of a lake or river.

If you are fishing a river, you would want to drop your jugs at the head of a pool. As the current moves the jugs through the pool, it is hoped that one would pass reasonably close to a hungry catfish. You should retrieve them at the other end of the pool before they pass over a series of ripples and out of sight.

A story comes out of Western Kentucky of two fishermen that have devised a system of jug fishing that really rakes them in. First of all, they own an electronic depth finder which is a very fine gadget in the hands of a knowledgeable fisherman. Their fishing is done almost exclusively by day and they proceed in the following manner.

They first move into a large cove of a lake and survey the bottom with the electronic depth finder. They look for coves where the water is in the 10 to 12 foot depth range. They fish only in coves where the wind is blowing across the lake toward the shore. They want the jugs to drift toward the shore--not out into the lake.

Their equipment consists of 50 jugs which they bait up all at the same time. They then start about mid-way of the cove and string a line of jugs from shore to shore. Next, they move a little further out into the lake and form another line of jugs and then a little further out and form a third line.

Occasionally they will have to set in the boat for awhile and wait for one of the jugs to start bobbing. But most of the time, before they get the 50 jugs in the water, one or two of the first ones they put in will be dancing a jig. On one occasion, they reported 7 of the jugs bobbing up and down at the same time.

The length of their line from jug to the hook is 10 feet. The factor that contributes to their success is this -- they take their bait to the catfish. By stringing three lines of jugs across the cove, the wind will blow the jugs toward the shore and practically every foot of that cove will have a piece of bait passing within a reasonably close distance. Also, they are taking advantage of the catfish's habitat. Remember, we mentioned that in the daytime, catfish move into deeper water and stay on the bottom. By using 10 foot lines, they were putting the bait near the bottom where the catfish were at. These two fishermen pointed out that their most successful time for doing this type of fishing was late August and September with October being the best month of all.

Like most everything else though, jug fishing can have its disadvantage if you let it get out of hand. One hapless fisher-

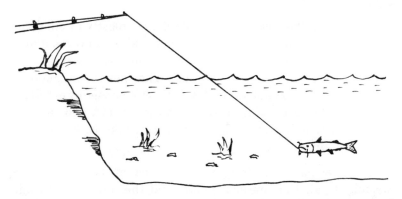

Catfish will often bite during the day but your chances for fast action are far better late in the evening and at night, usually from dusk until midnight.

man, so the story goes, experienced extreme disappointment anytime he pulled up a line without a fish. In an effort to overcome this severe frustration, he started floating the jugs half full of whiskey. If he caught a fish, he would simply string it, smiling happily as he did so. If he pulled up a line without a fish, it so depressed him that he would bury his disappointment by taking a nip from the bottle.

It worked beautifully for some time. He was coming home cheerful and happy whether he caught fish or not. But finally his wife got suspicious. One day she followed him to the lake and found that he had quit baiting the hooks. She made him give up fishing.

CHAPTER 10
BAITS

One could probably write a book on this one subject alone. Other than the carp, it's unlikely that any fish has been presented such an assorted offering of baits and concoctions as has the catfish. Almost every catfisherman seems to have his own personal bait recipe or some secret formula and many are very tight lipped when it comes to divulging their contents. You can hardly read the classified ad section of the outdoor magazines without noticing at least 3 or 4 "secret catfish bait recipes" for sale.

We mentioned earlier that catfish feed mostly by smell for he has a very sophisticated smelling apparatus. However, it also feeds to some extent by sight or by sensing sound waves for it will occasionally hit an artificial lure. They have been taken on plugs, jigs, spinners and even flies. But your catches by artificial lures are almost certain to be far and inbetween and there is probably not a fisherman living that can take catfish consistantly by lures alone.

Catfish baits could roughly be divided into two groups, one we might call the "natural baits" and the other the "recipe baits". Let us first devote some attention to the natural baits, then we'll probably get carried away when we start on some of those recipe baits.

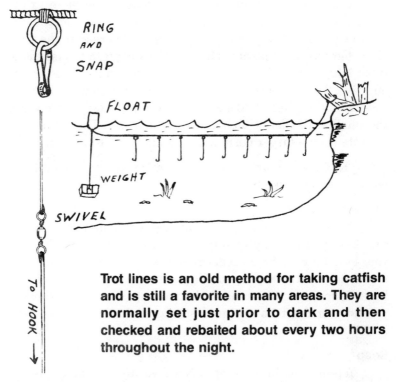

RING
AND
SNAP

FLOAT

WEIGHT

SWIVEL

To Hook ⟶

Trot lines is an old method for taking catfish and is still a favorite in many areas. They are normally set just prior to dark and then checked and rebaited about every two hours throughout the night.

One of the all time favorites, and I can assure you it will still take catfish today, is the common earthworm. About the only comment one could make regarding the earthworm is to put a big gob of them on your hook. The catfish has a big mouth so a big offering will obviously be more attractive than a single worm.

Another natural bait that has led to the downfall of many a catfish is the minnow. In fishing a minnow for crappie, bass and most other species, you want the liviest minnow you can find to attract their attention. Not so with Mr. Whiskers. Whether it's a minnow or an earthworm, it makes little difference to the catfish if it is alive or dead.

Other natural baits that will take catfish are frogs, toads, snails, mussels, shrimp, cut up fish, liver, beef, most all worms, clams, crawfish and crawfish tails, grasshoppers, crickets and most all other insects.

And now, let us take a look at some of the more"exotic baits"that will attract Mr. Catfish. Again let us touch on the fact that the catfish has a super sensitive smelling organ in the form of his barbels or whiskers. These barbels contain thousands of taste buds and it is for this reason that stink baits are so effective. That, plus the fact that the catfish is simply not very fussy about his diet. He'll eat most anything, most anytime. So, the smellier (if there's such a word), the better. They will draw the cats from a larger perimeter than non-smelling baits.

The following are some of the baits that have found favor with various Catfish fishermen.

Chicken Entrails

Believe it or not, this is a standard bait in many sections of the country. You can probably obtain an adequate supply from your local butcher. Some fishermen like to put them in a sack for 2 or 3 days until they ripen. How you would put these on the hook, I wouldn't think should be too important. But whether you have or don't have a good strong stomach would be very important.

Soap

Yep—just plain old soap. It's a favorite with many fishermen. Cut the soap in small sections and bury the hook in one. It takes the soap a long time to dissolve in the water and the catfish usually swallows the whole thing.

Sponge Rubber Bait

Cut some sponge rubber in small pieces. Make a mixture of rancid fish, cheese or ground beef then soak the sponge rubber pieces in it and use them for bait.

Blood Baits

This is a rather unusual bait. As to whether it is superior to the other baits or not would be debatable. To make this bait, simply take some animal blood, such as chicken blood, and mix it with pieces of cotton and let it harden.

Peanut Butter Bait

Take some flour and moisten it with hot water. Add an equal part of peanut butter, mix it, then divide into small balls.

154

This mixture will stay on your hook quite nicely and makes a very effective bait.

Paste Cheese Bait

Take a pint of corn meal and add 1 quart of boiling water. Cook over a low heat, stirring to keep the meal from sticking. As you stir, add small chunks of rancid cheese. Continue stirring until the mixture has the consistency of rubber and can be rolled around the pan. Now, place it on a board that has been sprinkled with corn meal then knead the dough. Add small pieces of cotton until the dough is quite tough and rubbery. Remove small quantities and roll into small balls. They can be kept fresh by keeping them rolled up in a damp cloth. If you wish, you may substitute sardines in place of the cheese.

Doughballs

One of the favorites among many fisherman is the doughball. They are all made pretty much by the same procedure but with any number of various scents. Take some rancid meat or cheese and mix it with flour and water to form a dough. Then mix in some cotton wool to make the dough thick and tough. For variety you can add any of the following scents; onion oil, celery seed oil, garlic oil, rhodium oil, tincture of asofoetida, anise oil, honey, vanilla, molasses, syrup, sugar, etc.

Cereal Bait

Take a box of cereal flakes, such as Corn Flakes, 2 cups of cottonseed meal, 2 tablespoons vanilla extract and 1/2 cup of warm water. Mix these together to form a soft dough. Sprinkle about one teaspoon of cinnamon over the dough and store in a plastic bag until ready for use.

Vegetable Bait

Take some oats, wheat or barley and add a quantity of green peas, corn and lima beans. Soak this mixture for a spell in enough water to form a thick paste, then boil until partially cooked. Allow the mixture to sour, then add one heaping tablespoon of bicarbonate of soda. When fishing, put a small amount over the barb of the hook only, preferably a No. 8 or No. 10 hook and fish just off the bottom.

Another Cheese Bait

Take 1 cup cornmeal, 1 cup flour, 1/2 cup oatmeal, 1 teaspoon sugar and 1/4 cup canned grated cheese. Mix these together, then add enough cold water to form a thick dough. Kneed the dough and roll into small balls.

In a separate pan, boil some water with a chopped onion in it, then drop the doughballs into it. When the doughballs begins to float, they are done. Cool them and place in a sealed glass jar. They will keep for several days.

Jello Baits

In one bowl, mix 1 cup cornmeal, 1/2 cup of flour and 1/2 package of strawberry jello.

In a separate pan, mix 2 tablespoons sugar, 1 teaspoon vanilla, dash garlic salt with 1 cup of water. Bring to a boil. Now add the dry ingredients and let them boil for a few minutes until mixture can be worked into a ball. Allow to cool, then pinch off small chunks and knead into small balls. Store them in a plastic bag.

The list of baits is almost endless. Catfish have also been caught on such things as hominy, kernels of corn, cockroaches and heaven knows what else. Then there are the special bottled scents that can be bought. According to the advertisements, they are suppose to work wonders. Just put a few drops of their product on your bait and they claim you will catch fish like crazy. Many of these so called "miracle scents" are nothing more than fish oil. But as you can see, the catfish has established quite a reputation for the various and sundry things he will eat.

CHAPTER 11
TRICKS THAT TAKE CATFISH

We normally think of the successful fisherman as the fellow who hops into his boat and takes off to various points in the lake hoping to locate a few catfish hangouts. But there are a couple of ways in which you can make the catfish come to you.

One method is called chumming and it can be very effective for generating some fast action. It is nothing more than chopping some unwanted fish into small pieces and then scattering the bits and pieces over an area you wish to fish. Throw the head, entrails and all into the water. Within a short while, the odor of those chopped up fish should have catfish swarming into the area providing you with a ball.

For chumming to be successful, it is necessary that you scatter the fish in calm water where the pieces will settle to the bottom in the general area of where you throw them. If there is a current, the pieces will be washed away defeating what you are trying to accomplish.

Baits suitable for chumming can be easily obtained. Almost every lake or stream has an abundance of small bluegill that are not large enough to bring home. In many cases they never will be because they are such prolific breeders that they often over populate a lake with the result that all remain stunted because there simply is not enough food. You will be doing your lake a favor by removing as many of these fellows as possible to allow better growth for those remaining. A No.10 hook baited with a very small earthworm or waxworm will usually nail several bluegill in short order. I am thinking of bluegill in the 4 to 5 inch range. These are too small to bring home, too large to use as bait for the normal size catfish, but they are just right to chop up for chumming.

Another somewhat similar trick that will obtain the same results is to get a sack of about 25 to 50 pounds, though size is not important. Fill the sack with such items as soybean meal, cottonseed meal or, if you can take it, chicken entrails. If you use the chicken entrails you might as well do it right -- and the right way is to leave the entrails in a big bucket or lard can until they are thoroughly ripened. A good way to tell when they are ripe is to set the bucket out in the back yard. In a few days you will get a call from one of your neighbor's threatening to notify the health inspector. This is a sure sign they are ready.

Take your sack of soybean meal or entrails, whichever the case may be, to the desired area you wish to fish and let it settle to the bottom. Leave the sack there for at least one full day. When you return, catfish should be milling around by the dozens trying to get into that sack of goodies.

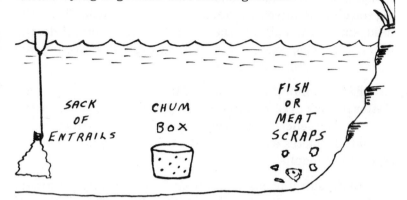

SACK OF ENTRAILS

CHUM BOX

FISH OR MEAT SCRAPS

You can make the catfish come to you. Any of the above methods will have the catfish flocking to your fishing area looking for a free meal.

A chum box is a plastic carton filled with meat, then punched with holes to allow the odors and flavors to escape.

If you had so desired, you could have left a cord tied to the sack attached to a bobber. This would have allowed you to retrieve the sack with its contents of raring-to-go bait. However, you may find that the ripened entrails won't stay on your hook. If so, make a small bag out of nylon stocking material, fill it with the entrails, then place it on the hook.

Another trick that should not be overlooked is to find out what is on the catfish's menu for that day and try to offer him that particular item. This is an easy thing to learn but it is contingent upon you first catching a catfish. Then simply perform an autopsy on his tummy to see what he has been eating.

One fisherman reports of the time he and his earthworms were having a rather bad day of it. The catfish simply weren't biting. Finally he managed to nail one of about a pound and immediately cut it open to find that this particular catfish had been dining on grasshoppers. This prompted a foot hike through the tall grass along the shore where he quickly bagged several grasshoppers. He started catching catfish as fast as he could throw in his line. On other days, it would probably be some other item rather than the grasshopper. The only way to find out is to perform an autopsy.

CHAPTER 12
RECIPES FOR CATFISH

Although the catfish may be ugly as home made soap and has an indiscriminating eating habit that matches his ugly hide, he is nevertheless quite tasty and is especially prized in our Southern States. He can be prepared in a number of ways and I would recommend that for a little variety you try two or three of the following recipes.

DEEP FRIED CATFISH

It's unlikely that all the fancy sauces and exotic spices will ever improve this old time favorite. After the fish has been dressed, roll it in cornmeal, coating it inside and out. Sprinkle lightly with salt and pepper. They fry in deep fat until done. Serve with hush puppies.

The oil should be about 360 to 370 degrees. This is important for if it is not hot enough, the meat can become greasy. A quick test to determine if it is hot enough is to drop a small piece of bread in the grease. If it browns within 40 seconds, it is hot enough.

HUSH PUPPIES

3-1/3 cups cornmeal
1-1/4 cups flour
2 tablespoons baking powder
2 teaspoons salt
3/4 teaspoon pepper

3 large eggs
1-1/4 cups milk
2/3 cup finely chopped onions
1/2 cup vegetable oil

First, sift the dry ingredients together. Then mix the eggs, milk, onions and fat. Add this to the dry ingredients and stir until blended. Form into small balls, about 2 inches in diameter, and deep fry at 350 degrees for 3 to 4 minutes or until golden brown.

BACON GRILLED CATFISH

Wrap the cleaned catfish in strips of bacon. Grill in a folding wire broiler or toaster over hot charcoal or wood coals. Serve it hot when the bacon is done and the fish becomes flakey.

BACON FLAVORED CATFISH

Put the cleaned catfish in a baking pan. Season with salt and pepper and cover with strips of bacon. Add 2 tablespoons of white wine and 2 tablespoons of water for each fish. Bake in a moderately hot oven until done. The flesh should flake easily.

Serve as is, or with a sauce made up of mayonnaise, finely chopped sweet pickles, a dash of lemon juice and a small amount of catsup.

CATFISH GUMBO

1 pound catfish fillets (skinned)
1/2 chopped green pepper
1 clove finely chopped garlic
1/2 cup celery (chopped)
1/2 cup onion (chopped)
2 beef bouillon cubes

1/4 cup vegetable oil	2 teaspoons salt
2 cups boiling water	1/4 teaspoon pepper
1 16 oz. can tomatoes	1/4 teaspoon thyme
1-1/2 cups hot cooked rice	1 whole bay leaf
1 10 oz. package of frozen Okra	Dash hot pepper sauce

Cook the green pepper, garlic, celery and onion in the vegetable oil until tender. Dissolve the bouillon cubes in the boiling water then add it, the tomatoes, okra and various seasoning to the first mixture, cover and simmer for 30 minutes. Add the fish, cover and simmer for an additional 15 or 20 minutes or until the fish is done. It should flake easily. Remove the bay leaf. Serve over the hot rice.

CATFISH AU GRATIN

Cook 2 pounds of catfish in boiling water until done. Remove. Save 2 cups of the fish stock. Flake the fish and remove all bones.

In a pan melt 3 tablespoons of butter and 4 tablespoons of flour to make a roux. Add teaspoon salt, the 2 cups of fish stock and 1 cup milk. Blend well and cook until smooth. Add 1-3/4 cups of grated cheddar cheese and 1/4 cup of Parmesan cheese. After the cheese has melted, fold in the flaked fish. Place in Au Gratin dishes. Sprinkle buttered bread crumbs over each dish. Place under broiler until browned.

WESTERN FRIED CATFISH

6 dressed catfish　　　　**2 tablespoons milk**
2 eggs　　　　　　　　　　**2 cups cornmeal**

Salt and pepper the fish to taste. Add the milk to the beaten eggs and stir. Dip the fish in the milk an egg batter and then roll in the cornmeal. Pan fry in hot fat until brown on one side. Turn and brown the other side until done.

BROILED CATFISH

6 dressed catfish　　　　　　**1 finely chopped clove garlic**
1/3 cup soy sauce　　　　　　**1/2 teaspoon ginger**
3 tablespoons vegetable oil　**1/2 teaspoon salt**
1 tablespoon liquid smoke　　**lemon wedges**

Mix all ingredients except the lemon wedges to form a sauce. Brush inside of the fish with the sauce and place them on a baking pan. Then brush outside with sauce and place under the broiler for about 5 minutes, basting occasionally. Turn the fish and broil another 5 minutes, until done, basting occasionally. Serve with the lemon wedges.

CATFISH STEW

5 pounds of catfish
2 tablespoon butter
2 tablespoons chopped celery
2 tablespoons chopped onion
1/4 teaspoon salt
1/4 teaspoon pepper
1 pint milk

Boil the catfish for 5 minutes in 2 quarts of salted water. Throw the water away and then pick all meat from the bones of the fish and dice the meat into small pieces. Now place the diced meat into a pan and add all the other ingredients. Heat the mixture until it is piping hot but do not bring it to a boil.

CALIFORNIA CATFISH

4 pounds of catfish
2 cups of cooked rice
2 tablespoons minced onion
1 lemon
1/4 cup butter
1/2 teaspoon curry powder
parsley flakes
salt
pepper

Slice the catfish into one inch steaks and place in a well greased baking dish. Sprinkle lightly with parsley flakes, salt and pepper. In a separate bowl, mix the rice, minced onion and curry powder and then spread this mixture over the tops of the fish. Then over the top of this, add thin slices of lemon and the butter. Cover the bake dish and bake in your oven for 30 minutes at 350 degrees. Then place under a broiler for about 2 minutes to lightly brown the top.

ARKANSAS CATFISH

5 pounds catfish
12 slices of bacon
1/2 cup cornmeal
2 teaspoons paprika
1 cup flour
1/2 cup evaporated milk
1 tablespoon salt
1 teaspoon pepper

First, fry the bacon until crisp and then set it aside. Mix the cornmeal, paprika and flour in one bowl. In a different bowl, mix the milk, salt and pepper. Now dip the fish in the milk mixture, then roll them in the flour mixture and fry them in the bacon grease for about 4 minutes to each side. Drain them on a paper towel and serve with the bacon.

TENNESSEE CATFISH

5 pounds of dressed catfish
2 tablespoons cooking oil
2 tablespoons parsley flakes
1/2 cup tomato sauce
2 packages dry cheese - garlic salad dressing mix (3/4 ounce)
Grated Parmesan cheese

Mix all the ingredients except the Parmesan cheese. Take the mixture and brush a liberal application to the fish, both inside and out. Now place the fish in a greased bake dish and sprinkle with the Parmesan cheese. Let it stand for 30 minutes. Preheat your oven to 350 degrees, then bake for 30 minutes. For a finishing touch, place the fish to within three inches of your broiler and broil for two minutes until the tops of the fish are lightly browned.

LOUISIANA CATFISH

3 pounds of catfish
1 cup vegetable oil
2 cups sliced mushrooms
1 1/2 cups dry white wine
2 crushed bay leaves
1/2 teaspoon thyme
3 tablespoons parsley flakes
3 tablespoons lemon juice
1/2 cup chopped onions
salt and pepper to taste

Place the catfish in a bake dish. Mix all the other ingredients together to form a sauce and them pour the sauce over the fish. Bake in an oven for about 30 minutes, or until the fish flakes easily.

BARBECUED CATFISH

Take about 4 or 5 pounds of catfish fillets, place them in a bowl. Cover the fillets with your favorite barbecue sauce. Marinate them in the refrigerator for about one hour, turning the fillets about every 20 minutes. Now take the fillets from the bowl and lay them on a sheet of aluminum foil. Broil them in your oven, allowing about 4 minutes per side. The fish are done when they begin to flake easily.

CHAPTER 13
GENERAL INFORMATION

Catfish are found all over the world with South America having the largest number of different species. They go by such names as walking catfish, blind catfish, armored catfish, talking catfish, toothless catfish, electric catfish, parasitic catfish, climbing catfish plus many others. In some parts of the world, they reach weights of over 400 pounds.

In the United States there are 28 different species. The smallest is the madtom which may grow no larger than one inch. The largest is the blue catfish which can reach a weight of 150 pounds. From the standpoint of popularity, they can be broken down into 4 groups; the blue cat, channel cat, bullhead, and flat head. We will touch briefly on each.

CHANNEL CAT

If a popularity count were to be taken, the channel cat would probably win. He is the only one in the catfish family to be classified as a gamefish. He can be caught on all types of live baits and occasionally various artificial lures. The average channel cat caught by fishermen is in the 2 to 4 pound range. He can, however, attain a maximum weight of 60 pounds. Basically, the channel cat is a stream fish but he has adapted very well to suitable lakes. He cannot tolerate pollution but instead demands well oxygenated water. As a youngster, he has black spots along his somewhat silvery side. The spots disappear with age and the very old ones turn inky black. He will have between 24 to 29 anal rays and a deeply forked tail. He is found throughout the United States and is farmed intensively in our southern states.

BLUE CAT

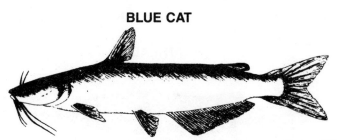

The blue cat is found primarily in our larger rivers. They have attained weights of 150 pounds though the average one caught would be in the 20 to 30 pound range. He is an excellent tasting fish and the most popular method for taking the blue is by jugging, which we described in an earlier chapter. The blue cat has between 30 to 36 anal rays and like the channel cat, has a deeply forked tail. Color wise, his upper half is a silvery pale blue with the lower half a milk-white. He prefers clear swift streams with a gravel bottom.

BULLHEAD

The bullheads are a hardy group that can live most any-where – turbid water, large lakes, small ponds and streams, even polluted water. There are several species such as the black bullhead, brown bullhead, yellow bullhead, etc. None of the bullheads grow too large. They have been recorded up to 7 pounds but the average one caught is less than one pound. From this standpoint, it is commercially the least important of the catfish we have discussed. The number of anal fin rays varies from 17 to 27, depending on the species. They are primarily bottom feeders and can easily be caught on worms and the various scent baits. As mentioned, they are hardy fish. In the winter, when other fish are suffocating, they will bury them-selves in the mud in semi-hibernation and emerge in the spring unharmed. They will also bury in the mud when ponds dry up and remain alive until the rains fill the pond up again.

FLATHEADS

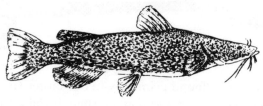

These fish are easily recognized by their broad flat head, a projecting lower jaw and large adipose fin. They have a short anal fin with 14 to 17 rays. They favor long, deep pools with slow currents. He feeds mostly at night and his favorite food is something fresh such as frozen shrimp or something alive such as a carp, bluegill or a small catfish. They rarely take baits with an odor. They can attain weights in the 100 pound area but your normal catch will be in the 3 to 30 pound range. Incidentally, if you want to go after some flatheads in the 50 to 100 pound range, one of the best baits you can use is another catfish of about 10 pounds. This from an aquatic biologist who has performed a few autopsies and should know. If you're like me though, I have enough problems getting in a 10 pounder. I'm not sure I would want to gamble him away on one of those big fellows.

The four catfish we have just discussed are the most popular for the American angler. There is another one that is making quite a name for himself though he's not too high on the popularity list. It seems that an aquarium shop in Florida had imported this species from Asia and one night they got up and walked out. Biologist became frantic and tried to control them by poisoning lakes they were known to inhabit. It did little good. They quickly swam to shore and then walked over to the next lake leaving the fish behind to die. This particular species, clarius batrachus, known as the walking catfish, has a rudimentary lung enabling it to breath air. It walks much like a person that was pulling himself over the ground with his elbows. Once he moves into a lake, he soon becomes the dominating species. Only time will tell as to how serious a threat he presents to anglers of other fish.

CHAPTER 14
CATFISH FARMING

In recent years, catfish farming has become a big business in many of our southern states. They are raised in ponds ranging from 60 to 100 acres. The ponds are all man-made usually scraped out by a bulldozer. It is essential that wells be near by to give the pond a constant supply of flowing water to provide the necessary oxygen to maintain the crowded fish population.

Fish farming began in the 1950's in Arkansas with the attempt to farm buffalo fish. This was soon abandoned because it took over a year to grow the fish to market size.

However, the interest was revived when farmers learned that the channel catfish would grow from a fingerling to market size within a year. They are fed daily on pellets made of fish meal, soybean meal and alfalfa. The market size of their catfish in December is about 2 pounds.

But, in all probability, it is not as easy or as much fun as it sounds. Catfish farmers say it is just as confining as raising dairy cattle, you have to be there every day. And they report, as in any other business, there are occasional failures. A crop could be wiped out by disease or an oxygen failure. The farmers report that when things go right, they get about the same return per acre of catfish as they do per acre of rice. The catfish are sold to restaurants and other retail outlets. Also, to the pay lakes up North.

Which brings up one final subject. Around many of our metropolitan and heavily populated areas, pay lakes have been growing at a quite rapid pace. I've seen some that were rather pathetically mismanaged. Trash of various sorts would line the shore, which is enough to discourage a fellow from fishing the water, much less eat the fish if he caught any.

Happily, not all pay lakes fit this description. Some are well managed and frequently stocked with a variety of fish. Most all are occasionally stocked with catfish. So, if there are no good catfish waters close by, a good pay lake may provide some short range enjoyment while you plan for that next big fishing trip.

At any rate, I am hopeful this little catfish study will help your future trips to be more productive and enjoyable.

CARP BY THE CARLOAD

CHAPTER 1
WHY FISH CARP ANYWAY

If a popularity contest should ever be held among our millions of American anglers as to their favorite fish, there is an excellent possibility the carp would have last place all to himself.

This is unfortunate.

It sometime seems that we have forgotten what fishing is all about. Basically, it was meant to be fun. Right? Yet we see large numbers of our fishing friends spend vast sums of money on all sorts of fancy fishing gear, take long expensive trips in quest of a particular fish, then often come home with very little to show for their efforts.

I certainly don't mean to imply that something may be wrong in going after a specific fish such as bass or trout. On the contrary. Bass and trout are among the most exciting of our fresh water fish. But to my way of thinking, pulling in a big stubborn fighting carp is a lot more fun than NOT pulling a bass. Good bass waters are not that abundant. Frequently, one must drive a long distance just to find a good bass lake. There are too many occasions when the long trip, the expense and the lack of bass makes one wonder if the fun you had was really worth it.

Not so with carp. He is one of the most abundant of American fishes. Good carp waters are within easy reach of most Americans. In the big majority of cases, the average person would have excellent carp waters within a few minutes of his home.

So why do we turn our noses up at carp? He is a fish with brute strength and is a stubborn fighter that will provide the angler with plenty of thrills. Properly prepared, he is a good tasting fish and a smoked carp is a downright delicacy. Yet we continue to snub the fellow. Why?

Apparently it is because fishermen are unwilling to discard the old handed-down prejudices that carp live mostly in polluted waters, they are low in food value and they are a non-game fish. However, these things are completely false. Carp can and do thrive in clean water, they are an excellent food fish and quite nutritious and I will guarantee you they can provide you with far more excitment when hooked than many of our so called game fish.

What we need to do is take a new, unbaised look at "Old Puckermouth." It could open up a completely new fishing world for the average American angler.

In England, the carp ranks second only to the trout as the most popular fish. In Europe, he is prized by both the commercial and sport fishermen. In Asia, the carp is considered King of Fishes. Emperors have been known to keep carp as pets in hugh tanks lined with jewels. And the carp is highly valued in Japan—the larger the fish the greater its value.

It may come as a surprise to many anglers that Izaak Walton was an avid carp fisherman. He referred to the carp as the "Queen of Rivers." In his book, The Complete Angler, which was written in 1653, he describes the various methods for taking carp which we will cover in a later chapter. It would seem that Sir Izaak was well aware of and appreciated the fighting ability of the carp, something that many modern day anglers have not yet discovered.

Carp were first introduced into America in 1877 and since then have spread completely across the country. Catches have already been made of well over 50 pounds and it is nothing unusual at all to pull them out in the 10 to 15 pound range. They are extremely abundant and it is reasonably certain that within a short drive of almost anybody's home will be waters that contain carp. And to make it even more enjoyable, they are relatively easy to catch.

It is a known fact that carp have some undesirable characteristics. They uproot aquatic vegetation with a result of destroyed waterfowl habitat, they muddy the waters of rivers and lakes, they destroy the eggs of game fish and they are quite prolific, to the point they can crowd out other game fish.

So, what should we do. We've already tried to seine them, we've tried netting them, we've tried gigging them, we've shot them with bow and arrow, we've tried poisoning them and we've called them every cuss word in the dictionary plus a few that aren't listed. And we've still got carp—by the millions.

They were here long before any of us arrived and they're still going to be here long after we are gone. It would now seem that about the only thing left is to learn to tolerate the fellows. The fact that carp have these undesirable traits should only give the angler that much more reason to want to do battle with as many of them as possible.

Mostly though, what the carp needs is a good public relations man. He is here and many of our waters already have heavy carp populations. There is nothing we can do to change it. It is much too late to argue whether he should have been introduced to America or not.

Our only alternative is to make the best of it. That is one of the purposes of this book—to present the carp for exactly what he is with the hopes that we can develop an appreciation for his better side.

Secondly, and more important I think, fishing for carp can be fun. But, like the pursuit of any fish or game, the more you know of your quarry, his habitat, his eating habits, etc.; the more fun you are going to have because the more successful you are almost certain to be.

As for myself, I don't really care what's hanging on at the other end of my line just so long as he is tugging, running and fighting to get off. If your fishing here lately hasn't been as enjoyable as it should be because the bass or trout were too far and inbetween, take a crack at some of those big carp there in your neighborhood waters. It just might put the fun back into fishing.

CHAPTER 2
HISTORY OF THE CARP

Asia apparently has the honor of being the original home of our present day carp. They were well established there many centuries ago and have been part of the national diets in China and Japan for over 2000 years. Records indicate thay were introduced into Europe around 600 A.D. where they proceeded to become quite popular. It would be over 1000 years later before they would find their way to America.

There is some confusion as to when the first carp reached the United States. One version has it that a Mr. J.S. Poppe of Sanoma, California had 83 carp shipped from Holstein, Germany in 1872. Only 6 survived the long trip and one other died when it was placed in the rearing pond. The other 5 were near death but soon revived and by the following May had grown from 6 inches to 16 inches and had already produced over 300 baby carp. All this in 10 months.

One other version has it that a Mr. Robert J. Pell of Pellham, New York had great numbers of carp as early as 1857. He had purchased them from a certain Captain Robinson of Newburgh, New York.

172

But regardless of who has the honor of introducing them, it was in 1877 that widepread distribution began when the U.S. Bureau of Fisheries entered the picture.

This time 345 carp were shipped from Hochst, Germany to Rudolph Hessel, a fish culturist for the United States Government. These fish were first stocked in ponds in Boston's Druid Hill. Within a short while, they became overcrowded and 113 of then were transferred to Babcock Lake in Washington, D.C.

The action was defended by Spencer F. Baird who was then United States Commissioner of Fish and Fisheries who wrote, "Their instinct for domestication has already been established—and there is no reason why time should be lost with less proven species."

Within a short while, Americans throughout the country were demanding breeding stock of the carp, a fish they literally knew nothing about. Government "experts" were making wild promises about the potentials of this newly introduced species.

Apparently the politicians of those days weren't much better than the ones we have today. Here was an opportunity to make a few points with the folks back home and they had no intention of allowing it to slip past them. They demanded and obtained stock for their congressional districts. In 1883, a total of 260,000 carp were distributed among 298 districts. Only three congressional districts failed to receive any. In an incredible short time, the ancestors from those oritinal 345 carp had spread from coast to coast.

Going back to A.J. Poppe, he later wrote, "Every fish that I can possibly send to market here sells readily at one dollar per pound. Farmers who have natural facilities on their places for making ponds and who have access to canals or rivers communicating with large cities, can greatly increase their income with but small trouble and expense.

There ought to be one person in every county who would raise choice carp as stock fish to sell to others to fatten for their own tables. It would be a cheap but sumptuous food and at the same time very convenient, as they are ready to be eaten at all times of the year."

When you consider these fish were bringing $1.00 per pound in the 1870's it gives you some idea as to their popularity at the time. That was several times higher than prime beef of that day.

By now, thousands of requests were coming from sportsmen who wanted the carp stocked in their area. And within a short time the populations explosion had started. In 1899, Milton Trautman wrote in his Fishes of Ohio, that 3.6 million pounds of carp were taken by commerical fishermen from Lake Erie. This only 20 years after the carp were first stocked in that lake.

Another populations explosion was taking place at the same time in the Illinois River. In the 1880's, the average commercial, catch of Buffalo fish was around one million pounds per year. Then the carp was introduced. By 1896, the commerical catch of carp was 22 million pounds. This gives you some ideal of their astronomical growth potential, at least compared to buffalo-fish. By 1912, it was reported that a 600 acre spawning area along the Illinois River contained 1.5 billion carp eggs.

With the fantastic growth of the prolific carp, it soon became apparent that problems were developing. In 1905, the U.S. Fish Commission assigned Leon Cole to investigate and this is part of his report. "As to the relation of carp to aquatic vegetation, the evidence seems to be pretty strong that in general they are very destructive, and are probably, in large part at least, responsible for great reduction of wild celery and wild rice that has been noted in many of our inland marches in the last few years...It must be admitted that where there is a comparatively large number of carp in a pond, the water is in an almost constant state of roitiness...The only practical remedy is removal of the fish."

Prince Edward of Canada wrote 15 years after carp had been introduced into that country, "German carp are nomadic in their habits and wander apparently aimlessly into all accessible waters, hence if introduced into any streams, will spread rapidly over the whole system...Like undesirable weeds, they have spread everywhere and it is practically impossible to limit their progress or to effect their extirpation."

Both gentlemen were correct. The carp had spread rapidly and was now the dominant fish in many of our lakes and streams. They did best in the fertile, shallow lakes. Many of the better suited waters were found to contain from 200 to 400 pounds of carp per acre of water.

It was soon learned that the carp could cause heavy and serious damage to a lake. They not only destroyed aquatic vegetation but would muddy the water by stirring up the sediment. The muddy water would reduce the penetration of light which retarded the growth of the submerged plants. It was believed that carp were also responsible for heavy algae growth in some lakes by their constant stirring of the bottom sediment which kept lake bottom nutrients in circulation to encourage algae growths. However, other fish with similar habits could also be guilty of this.

As the carp multiplied, it was noted that the weed beds declined and in many cases were replaced by bare mud. Lakes and ponds that were once clear now stayed cloudy with silt.

Tests were conducted to determine for certain if the carp was the villian or not. Fences were installed across various areas of water to prevent carp from entering. The results were spectacular. Inside the fence, the vegetation flurished. Outside the fence, the carp soon rooted up and destroyed the plants and weed beds. As long as the carp were allowed to remain, the water stayed turbid with little recovery of the vegetation. However, once the carp were removed, the water soon became clear and there was a noticeable increase in the waterfowl.

So, in a period of only a few years, the carp had gone from a hero with such great potential, to a villian that threatened to destroy much of our good fishing and waterfowl habitat. But, let us again note, scientific studies indicate that the carp is here to stay so we might as well start giving him some attention and make the most of it.

CHAPTER 3
NO WONDER HE'S A PROBLEM

Of all the fish in our American waters, the carp would have to rank as one of the hardiest. He will feed on almost anything that is edible. However, the major part of their diet is made up of insect larvae, crustaceans and small mollusks. They often uproot water plants with their vacuum type mouths.

Test have been conducted and it has been found that a very fat carp can go for one full year without a bite of food. But when it comes to eating, they are somewhat like a goat—they'll eat most anything in sight. It has been found that carp can get so fat that they will literally over-eat themselves to death.

Studies have been made by examining the stomachs of various carp. It was learned they will normally contain from 30 to 40 percent vegetable matter and 15 to 30 percent aquatic insects. Other items include waterfleas, eggs and small fry of other fish. Other studies indicate they are attracted to such items as beef bouillon, liver extract, tobacco juice, meat products, molasses and immitation maple flavor.

The carp is a hardy, durable fellow and can often survive in water that will not support other species. They can tolerate water temperatures ranging from 35 to 95 degrees. There are few other fish that can match that, if any. The pH factor is of little

When the waters drop below 50 degrees, carp will stop feeding. They will not start feeding again until the following spring when the waters again rise above 50 degrees.

concern to the carp. He appears to be perfectly contented in filthy water or water that is crystal clear. The carp rarely gets sick. Their life span is somewhat comparable to man. On the average, they live to be 75 or 80 years years old. The record is a carp in Japan that was over 200 years old when he expired.

Carp have a strong desire for survival. In addition to their ability to thrive in polluted waters and to withstand extreme water temperature change, they also require little oxygen and can survive for long periods out of water. In one study, two biologists force-fed 1600 different chemicals to carp under laboratory conditions. Out of the 1600 chemicals, only 135 killed all the carp tested.

The evidence is overwhelming that large concentrations of carp can cause serious damage to a lake. Not only do they eat game fish eggs and destroy their breeding grounds but they compete with other fish for the available food supply and often become the dominate species. They uproot aquatic vegetation and their constant roiling the water can keep it so muddy as to prevent the penetration of light to submerged plants, thus retarding their growth.

Hunters who rank the canvasback as king of waterfowl have an excellent reason to hate the carp. Some of the finest lakes in the country that once attracted massive flights of canvasback ducks have had their wild celery beds and pondweeds devestated by the carp.

Efforts to control the carp have fired the imagination of conservation agencies for decades. It has been found that in lakes where carp were completely wiped out, the lake made a rapid return to normal with a quick return of vegetation and pondweed. In other lakes, where large numbers of carp were removed, it was noted that game fish would quickly start to increase in numbers. This was effective though only in lakes that were seined heavily over a period of years.

Numerous methods have been tried to control or eliminate the carp. Thousands of dollars are spent each year in commercial netting operations that are designed to reduce the over-populated rivers and lakes. They employ such items as the hoop net, gill net and the seine, all of which require a commercial fishing license.

The seine has been quite effective in controlling carp in shallow lakes running 10 to 20 feet deep. In some such lakes, they have averaged anywhere from 130 to 430 pounds per acre each year. It was noted that in lakes which had an income of domestic sewage, these lakes had an unusual high yield of carp.

In the cool, deeper lakes, the carp population usually remain fairly small and they do little damage. Only in the shallow coves of such lakes is the damage even noticeable. Many of these lakes are difficult to seine and what few are removed are quickly replaced by new growing carp.

Screens and barriers have been erected to prevent carp from migrating upstream and populating new waters or waters where the carp have been removed. These have been successful to some extent. Another method that has proven effective is to lower the water in various man-made reservoirs during spawning season. Carp usually lay their eggs in the shallow waters of coves and sloughs. As the water is lowered, the eggs are exposed to the air destroying the hatch.

Another widespread practice for controlling the carp is through the use of various poisons. Taxaphene, rotenone and other chemicals have been used with success. Unfortunately, they are expensive with many side effects. Not only do they kill carp, but all other fish and lake life as well. If not used carefully, it can also result in the loss of birds and other wildlife.

The unfortunate aspect of all these methods is that while it may temporarily rid or reduce the carp population, it is just that—temporary. Fishermen themselves have already played a great part in the distribution of carp and they will continue to do so. Many fishermen use young carp for live bait, probably unintentional, but a fact nevertheless. When they buy or seine a bucket of minnows to go fishing, how many check to see if any of the minnows are carp. I doubt if the thought ever occured to the average fisherman. Many of these minnows escape, others are thrown in the water when the fishing is over and, of course, the population explosion starts all over again.

Which again brings up the point that carp are here and they are here to stay. And since they are, you might as well get the old fishing rod out and have a little fun.

CHAPTER 4
BUT HE DOES HAVE SOME GOOD POINTS

There is no question, when carp become overabundant, they can and do cause considerable harm. However, like most other living creatures, there are a few good things that can be said in the carp's behalf. For example, we do have some waters in this country that have literally become choked with excessive growth of vegetation, vines, weeds, etc. Carp can and have been used to control the growth of such vegetation.

Secondly, carp does have some commercial value though it is of no great importance. There are about 40 states where commercial netting of carp exist. Their dollar value is somewhere in the area of $1.5 million per year. Their heaviest concentration is in the mid-west. Around 16½ million pounds of carp are taken each year from the Mississippi River drainage and about 6 million pounds are taken in the eastern Great Lakes Region. The recent price has been around 4¢ per pound. That's quite a drop from $1.00 per pound they were bringing in the 1870's.

However, if the carp is ever to gain in popularity, it will be from his main asset which is sheer abundance. He is found most everywhere, he is easy to catch and he grows rapidly into a good size fish that can give the angler all the fight he wants.

As a youngster, I use to hop on my bike, peddle out to the edge of the small community where I was raised and within 15 or 20 minutes would be on the banks of a farm pond catching sunfish, perch, catfish and an occasional bass. I expect the majority of our over-40 population can make similiar statements. But the average youngster of today cannot.

179

With each passing year, our nation becomes more and more urbanized. City children of today do not have access to good fishing waters that were available only a few years ago. In many cases, lengthy and costly trips are necessary to find good fishing waters. In my opinion this is where the angler of today is missing a good bet by ignoring the carp.

There are few cities in the United States that do not have good carp waters nearby. Many of our cities were built on the banks of rivers that are abundant in carp. With the pollution problem of recent years, most fishermen have shunned these waters. But this is changing. We are making progress toward controlling pollution and it's about time we take another look at the angling potential existing at our doorstep.

I cannot think of a better fish for the average city dweller to pursue than the carp. By average, I mean a person who has neither the time or money to be taking lengthy fishing trips every week or so. Of course, there are exceptions. Some cities have excellent game-fish waters nearby. But in too many cases, even these waters are over fished and good catches of bass and other popular species are hard to come by.

If we city dwellers would modify or change our attitude toward "Old Puckermouth," it's quite possible that a majority of us could spend many a pleasant evening within 20 to 30 minutes of our home trying to entice the old fellow onto our line. He is such a prolific breeder, adapts to such a wide range of waters, is so abundant and grows so rapidly; that he is the ideal fish for the angler with limited access to good waters.

The common carp (cyprinus carpio) which is so abundant in America is a giant member of the minnow family. In terms of both species and numbers, they are our largest group of freshwater fishes.

They are among our fastest growing fish. In waters where food is abundant, a carp may grow to one pound during his first year. However, under normal circumstances, the average one-year old carp will weigh a ½ pound and measure around 9 inches in length. They will range from 15 to 18 inches by the second year. Reported catches have been made of carp in the 80 to 90 pound range, although these reports have been questioned by authorities. The recognized record for the United States is 55 pounds. Carp in the 5 to 10 pound range can be caught readily in waters throughout the United States.

The carp is not a wild, aerial acrobat as some other game fish but rather is more like a back-alley brawler who uses brute force to fight his battle. He will hang on like a bulldog and make runs and rolls that will put a highly respectable bend in your rod. If you are fishing with light tackle, treat him with the greatest of respect. He can furnish you with far more excitement than many of our popular game fish.

One should also not overlook the carp from the standpoint of its eating quality. They can be french fried, pan fried, broiled, baked or pickled. And a properly smoked carp is eating at its finest. If you have never tasted a smoked carp, be sure to try one at your first opportunity.

While we are saying a few nice things about the carp, let us also point out that in many cases, carp are sometimes blamed for a problem, when in fact, it should have gone to some other fish. Black bullheads, sheepshead, buffalo-fish, fresh water drum, etc., are all bottom feeders that possible contribute to some degree to the problems usually assigned to the carp.

We will again say that to simply cuss Old Puckermouth is of no great value. If you really want to help the situation, you can do so by taking more carp—and have a lot of fun while you are doing it.

CHAPTER 5
HABITAT

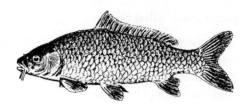

One of the most important aspects of consistant successful fishing is to have a basic knowledge of a particular fish's habitat. The more you know, the better will be your chances for succes. If you doubt this, just look at the statistics. It's a known fact that 10% of the fishermen catch 90% of the fish. Is this because those 10% are just lucky all the time? I can assure you that is not the reason.

Not too many years ago, the standard procedure for the average fisherman was to get an urge to go fishing, then simply pick up his gear and go. (I expect that still applys to many.) Sometimes he would catch a lot of fish. At a later date, he would return to that same spot and not catch a single fish. His only explanation would be "They're not biting today." That may have been a correct accessment. But in all probability there was a more logical reason for his failure.

Some fish are known to stay only in shallow waters during particular seasons or at particular times of the day or night. At other times they move to deep waters. Some fish will strike any kind of a lure during spawning season. Other fish will not hit at all while spawning. Some fish bite better at night, others early of a morning. The more we know of when and where a fish is most likely to be feeding, the greater will be our opportunities. Let us now examine the carp in greater detail to further our knowledge of this rugged fellow and some of his characteristics.

The carp is a member of the family cyprinidae. It is classified as genus Cyprinus, species carpio. The three most common

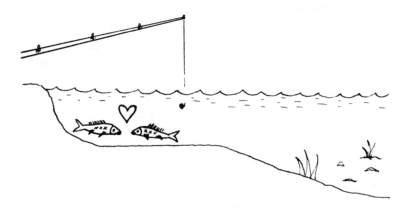

Carp do not feed while they are spawning. Your best bet during this period is to concentrate on crappie, bluegill or some other species until the carp get through their love making duties. After spawning, carp again start to feed.

kinds of carp are the Scale Carp, Mirrow Carp and Leather Carp. Scale carp are covered evenly with scales. Mirrow-carp have larger scales of different sized. Leather carp have only a few scales and look almost bare. All carp are characterized by a long dorsal fin and two barbels on each side of the upper jaw.

Carp prefer warm-water lakes or ponds and slow-moving rivers. They like weedy places with a muddy bottom. They are omnivorous, but one of their favorite foods is apparently the midge larvae which inhabits the mud of lake bottoms. It is during their efforts to obtain these larvae from the bottom of their habitat that carp roil the water which increases turbidity with its adverse effect on many plants and animals.

There are two periods during the year when carp do not feed. When the water temperature drops below 50 degrees they quit eating and become quite inactive. Obviously, there would be no point in chasing carp during the winter. Also, they do not feed during spawning season. This is rather flustrating because often you can see their backs exposed during spawning so there is no question as to where to toss your bait. But it will do no good. His mind is on matters other than food. However, the carp spawning season can be an exciting time for the bow and arrow enthusiast.

183

As we have just mentioned, carp remain dormant all winter. But in the spring, when the waters start to warm up, they move into the shallows with a ravenous appetite. Now is the time to start applying your knowledge of the carp's feeding habits. When the spring waters reach temperatures between 55 to 60 degrees is an excellent time to fish the shallows. For even greater success, sprinkle the fishing area the night before with field corn. This will attract large numbers of carp. You can use soaked grains of corn for bait and have yourself a barrell of fun.

In the late spring and early summer, when the water temperatures rise to between 58 and 68 degrees, the carp move into shallow bays, stream tributaries or flooded plains and start to spawn. The most ideal temperature for spawning is around 62 degrees.

They usually scatter their eggs about, normally in small groups of 500 to 600 eggs on vegetation, rubble and debris. One female may lay anywhere from 1,000,000 to 3,000,000 eggs. The eggs are slightly adhesive and stick to the vegetation and debris or sink to the bottom. They will hatch in four to ten days, depending on water temperature. Unlike most other fish that stand guard over their eggs until they hatch, the carp does nothing to stop predation. From the eggs that are not eaten by other fish soon emerge the baby carp. After about four or five days the yolk sac of the tiny carp has been used up and within 2-1/2 weeks, the young carp has grown to a length of one inch and they now migrate into deeper waters. They will normally grow from six to nine inches within the first year although in fish ponds with controlled temperature and proper food, they can easily exceed 14 inches the first year. Their growth is far greater during the warm season. Once the water temperature drops below 50 degrees, growth apparently stops and does not resume until the following spring. They reach sexual maturity during their second year and often live from 40 to 80 years. They have reached weights above 50 pounds and it is not unusual to take one in the 25 to 30 pound range.

In fish ponds with controlled temperatures, etc., carp will produce more than 1,000 pounds per acres. It is said that the fast growing pond-cultured carp have a superior taste.

After spawning season, carp again start to feed and can be taken throughout the summer and fall until the water temperature again drops below 50 degrees. Here are some of the times and places one would be most likely to find carp during the summer and fall.

Shortly after the spawning season, carp like to spend the early morning hours along the river and lake banks. Just after the sun rises, you can stalk along the banks and look for carp rolling in the weeds and mud. Pay close attention because often only a fin or tail will be visible.

If you see a carp, toss your bait well beyond the fish so as not to spook him. Then slowly reel the bait back toward the fish.

On days when the water is clear you can frequently see the carp take the bait and start to run. No need for any guess work here. When he starts to run, sock it to him.

As summer approaches, the carp's feeding pattern becomes somewhat eradict. But with a knowledge of this pattern, one can predict with a fair degree of accuracy when and where he will be feeding. All indications suggest that changes in the water temperature determines when and where the carp will start or stop feeding.

It would be well to note that carp feed most heavily in waters with a temperature between 60 and 70 degrees. Remember those figures—60 to 70 degrees. This means that at some periods of the day or night, carp will be feeding in the shallows, at other times they will be in the deep. An inexpensive water thermometer and a knowledge of how to use it is one of the finest assets a carp fisherman can have.

Carp will feed all night but only under certain conditions. When temperatures in the shallows hang in at slightly above 60 degrees, carp will normally stay there and feed in the shallows all night. However, when the temperature drops below 60 degrees in the shallows, they will move into deeper water. If the temperature in the deeper water is about 60 degrees or slightly over, they will again feed all night. However, when the deep water drops below 60 degrees, they will simply seek the warmest water in the lake and cease feeding until the following day. There is not much else that can be said regarding night fishing for carp. Your thermometer will tell you whether to fish the shallows, or whether to fish the deep or whether to go home and try some other time.

Because the shallows are usually too cool at night, carp will spend the majority of those nights in deeper water. As dawn approaches, they start moving toward the shallows on the western side of the lake, the side which receives the first sunlight. At the first light of dawn, many will move into the shallows. They apparently do this more by habit than anything else for they do not start feeding since the water is still too cool.

The most ideal time for taking carp is when the water temperature is between 60 and 70 degrees. During the summer and fall, you should always look for this temperature range to get the best action.

As the water warms up, the carp becomes more active and some leaping will be observed. When it reaches the 60 degree mark, they start to feed and will continue to do so throughout the day until the water becomes too warm, usually above 70 degrees. They now cease feeding but will remain in the warm waters of the shallows for the balance of the day. Frequently, they can be seen wallowing or swimming about in the shallows but if it's very much above 70 degrees, they won't bite. In the evening when the temperature starts to fall, the leaping will again be observed. When it drops to around 70 degrees, the carp start on another feeding spree. As the sun sets, there is usually a general movement of carp to the east side of the lake, again to get the last effects of the sun's warmth. They continue feeding until the water becomes too cool when they now move back to the warmer deep water.

This chapter on the habitat of the carp is quite important. Regardless of how effective a carp bait you are using, if you aren't putting it where Old Puckermouth is at and at the right time, you simply aren't going to catch any. On the other hand, if you can consistently toss your bait into the vicinity of where the carp is feeding, you will increase your chances for success enormously.

At the risk of over-simplication let me quickly summarize these last few paragraphs because this information is extremely important to the serious carp fisherman.

Carp do not feed in the winter when the water is below 50 degrees. They feed ravenously in the spring in shallow waters when the waters warm above the 55 degree mark. They start spawning when the water temperature reaches around 60 degrees. They do not feed during the spawning period. After spawning, and for the remainder fo the summer and fall, carp seek a water temperature that ranges between 60 and 70 degrees. They stop feeding if the water temperature goes very much above or below those two figures. In the early morning, carp feed on the west side of the lake (if the water temperature is between 60 and 70 degrees), in the evening on the east side. Learn to use your water thermometer. Remember that the temperature of deep water changes very slowly, the temperature of shallow water will change more rapidly. Check the temperature in the shallows. If it is between 60 to 70 degrees, this is where the carp will most likely be feeding. When it drops below 60, move to the deeper waters until you again find the 60 to 70 degree temperature range. One final note. The evidence seems to suggest that when carp start leaping, usually early in the morning and late in the evening, they are just getting ready to start on a feeding spree.

CHAPTER 6
TACKLE AND TECHNIQUE

The tackle you would select for carp should be no different than what you would use for most any other fish. Of course many a carp has been hoisted from the water on a cane pole. However, much of the fun of fishing is lost by this method. You are limited by the waters you can cover whereas a spin-casing rod and reel will allow you to fish the deep and shallow waters from one spot.

One needs to give much thought to the type of rod and reel he should use in the pursuit of carp. I would imagine the average weight of the fish caught in the United States would be well under 5 pounds. Light fishing tackle with a 6 to 10 pound test are far best for these as they provide the maximum thrills for fish of this size. As long as you tangle with carp in the 4 to 6 pound range, light tackle would be your best choice. But the problem is that you never know when one of those bruisers will take your bait. Many a light fishing tackle outfit has failed to produce and occasionally they get busted up when a big carp latches on to the other end. It is pretty much up to the individual angler depending on the size carp he is seeking. Perhaps a fair compromise would be a medium size open-face reel with a line in the 10 to 16 pound test range.

Certainly the angler of today is in better shape than Sir Izaak Walton. His line was made from tapered horsehair. When he hooked a big carp, he would throw his rod in the water to keep the fish from breaking his line. Later, with the fish still on but weakened, he would retrieve his rod and finish the fight.

The size hook you use would again depend on the size carp you are after. It could range from a size No. 8 for small carp up to a No. 2. It's unlikely you would need anything larger. Tie the hook directly to the line. As in any other type of fishing, the hooks should always be kept extra sharp. Small hook files can be purchased that were designed for this specific task.

Many carp specialist fish without a bobber, simply allowing the bait to settle to the bottom. With this method, especially at night, it is necessary to hold the line loosely between the thumb and forefinger to detect a bite. If you use a bobber, it should be an extremely small one. If the bobber is large enough that the carp can detect any resistance when he bites, he will drop the bait.

The same is true for sinkers. No sinker should be used that will create any resistance when the carp takes the bait. A slip sinker is far best. It will lie on the bottom and as the fish starts to run with the bait, he will feel no resistance as the line slides through the eye of the sinker. You should probably tie a small object, such as a piece of match stick about 4 inches above the hook. This will prevent the sinker from sliding against the bait. One exception might be when fishing rivers with heavy currents. A sinker should be no great drawback in this situation.

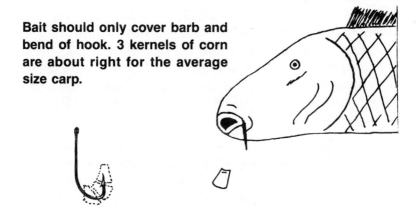

Bait should only cover barb and bend of hook. 3 kernels of corn are about right for the average size carp.

Carp do not attack a bait. They simply suck it in. For this reason your bait should be small. A pea size piece of bait is about right for the average size carp. OVERBAITING IS A COMMON PROBLEM AMONG MANY CARP FISHERMEN.

In fishing the open-faced reels, it is almost always best to leave the bale open. The carp should be allowed to run briefly with the bait without feeling any premature resistance. Just remember that carp are extremely sensitive to any resistance on the line, whether it be a sinker, cork or the line itself. When there is no resistance, they swim off confidently with the bait in their mouth enabling the angler to set the hook.

Learning when to set the hook is something that comes only with experience. The right time is when the carp has the bait and hook well in his mouth. This of course is far easier said than done. If you strike too soon, obviously you're going to miss him. If he toys with the bait and feels any kind of line resistance, he will immediately drop it. Experience will have to dictate when to strike. If they are running with the bait, you should set the hook within a moment or two after you are sure the run is underway. If they are simply toying with the bait and then ejecting it, you will need to try the "instant strike technique." This can best be done by looping the line over the index finger or holding it lightly between the thumb and forefinger of the left hand so you easily detect the slightest nibble at the other end.

There are other tackle and techniques used for taking carp which we will only touch on briefly. In some states you are allowed to spear carp during the spawning run. Be sure to check your state law before trying this. All that is needed is a five-pronged spearhead on a long wooden pole. Carp are also taken on set lines and multi-hook trotlines. Again, these are not legal in some states and with certain restrictions in other states. Be sure to check.

One final piece of tackle that should always be included is a landing net. For a margin of safety, it should be a fairly large size one. Be careful as you try to net him. Often, as the net is swooping toward him, the carp will roll and flap violently in a final effort at freedom.

It again only emphasises what we have been saying all along—that the carp is a fighter which has the capabilities of putting the fun back into fishing. Once you have hooked a few of these fellows, you just might get hooked yourself on fishing for carp.

CHAPTER 7
BAITS

With the exception of the catfish, it is doubtful that any other fish could rival the carp for the various baits that have been devised in his behalf. To describe what the carp will eat, you can do so in two words. Anything edible. Everything from bread, potatoes, corn, earthworms, marshmellows and doughballs have been tried and carp have been caught on everyone of them.

We will discuss several of these but first a very important word about bait fishing for carp. One should be aware that carp have no teeth like most other game fish. They do not attack a bait but rather, simply suck it in. For this reason your baits should be small. A pea size piece of bait is quite big enough for an average size carp. Overbaiting for carp is a common problem among many anglers. Obviously, the hook should also be small enough that is can be sucked in along with the bait. Of course the larger the fish you are seeking, the larger should be your hook and bait. The only drawback to using the larger baited hooks is that it will cause you to miss many of the more moderate size carp.

Carp are vegetarians by nature and they are fond of soft foods. He is endowed with a keen sense of smell, and can be attracted from a long distance by dropping most anything into the water that has a strong odor. Some old timers use to spit tobacco juice on their bait for this reason. At least one bait manufacturer claims they are attracted to color—especially to their blue doughbait. It would be debatable as to whether it is the color or the odor of the doughbait that draws the carp.

It would be well to again mention that carp are highly suspicious. Often they will pick up a bait, hold it momentarily and them drop it. Frequently they will do this several times. If you try to set the hook and miss, you will spook the fish. But once the carp is satisfied the bait is edible, he'll suck it into his mouth and start moving away. About 4 or 5 feet is all you need to give before setting the hook.

One could almost write a book on baits alone that have been designed for taking carp. Some fishermen have been known to dip their baits in mixtures made from molasses, honey, corn syrup or anise oil. Almost anything that has an odor has been tried at one time or another.

Peanut butter and flour blended with a little hot water is suppose to be irresistible to carp. It will stick on a hook the same way it sticks in the roof of your mouth.

Another bait is to use canned biscuit dough mixed with a little cotton to firm it up a bit. Various cereals, such as corn flakes, can be moistened enough to form soft balls. Also bread and condensed milk or soft limburger cheese mixed with bread is a very effective bait.

Other items that are often used are small marshmellows, gum drops, partially cooked potatoes, carrots, parsnips, green peas, corn, lima beans, worms, berries, tomatoes, minnows, crawfish, etc.

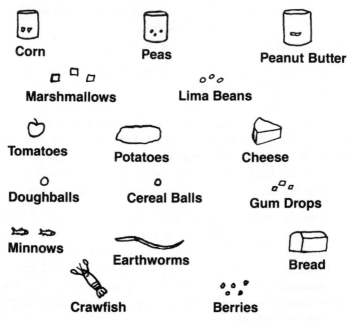

Corn   Peas   Peanut Butter

Marshmallows   Lima Beans

Tomatoes   Potatoes   Cheese

Doughballs   Cereal Balls   Gum Drops

Minnows   Earthworms   Bread

Crawfish   Berries

When it comes to eating, carp are somewhat like a goat— they'll eat most anything in sight. This is one of the reasons that most any bait you offer them will get results.

Various recipes have evolved that some anglers swear by. Most of these are doughball mixtures. Here is one that is quite popular. Put 6 teaspoons of sugar and 3 cups of water in a pan and bring to a boil. Then slowly add 2 cups of flour and 1 cup of yellow meal, stirring constantly until the mixture becomes a stiff ball—anywhere from 10 to 30 minutes. Remove and sprinkle with additional corn meal and start kneading it into a large ball. Wrap in wax paper and place it in the refrigerator. Pinch off in small balls when ready to use.

There are many variations of the doughball. For instance, to the preceding doughball recipe, you might add such items as sugar, molasses, aniseed, limburger cheese, corn syrup, licorice or most anything to give it a different flavor. Other doughball concoctions include mixtures such as corn flakes and strawberry jam rolled into small balls or honey and some type of cereal flakes pressed onto the hook.

One carp specialist has devised the following cereal doughball recipe that he naturally claims to be the best ever developed. Sometime you might want to try it to see if you agree. Take a cooked carrot and crush it. Add some sugar, cinnamon, peanut butter, corn and some corn flakes with a small amount of water. Boil for about 30 minutes or until it becomes firm and can be rolled into balls.

One of the big problems with doughball baits is that too many fishermen have a tendency to put too much on the hook. It is best to not cover the hook completely but rather cover only the barb and part of the bend in the hook. It should not cover the shank of the hook. We have mentioned that carp often just mouth a bait and then spit it out. This will happen frequently after a carp has just gorged himself. If you suspect this is happening, try placing a small bait that barely covers the hook barb, then try the instant strike the moment you feel the carp inspecting the bait.

However, for all the recipes and concoctions that have been devised for carp, many experts claim they are totally unnecessary. One successful carp fisherman of many years claims the only bait he will use is canned sweet corn. To start with, he will toss a handfull of corn over the area he plans to fish. This is called chumming and it soon has carp moving into the area to enjoy the feast. He then puts enough kernels of corn on a No. 8 hook to cover the barb and the bend and tosses it among the scattered corn. This particular angler usually allows the carp to run from 10 to 20 feet before setting the hook.

Another carp expert claims the only thing he ever uses is bread. He feels carp are too smart to take an unnatural bait, such as a stationary one hanging suspended from a bobber. He vows that a bait sinking slowly under its own weight is the effective way to take carp. His method is to press a small piece of bread around the barb and bend of a hook but leave the outer edge of the bread soft. When tossed onto the water, the bread will float briefly but as it absorbs water, it will slowly start to sink. He declares that on many an occasion, he has seen carp move a long distance to intercept his bread ball.

One final bait we will touch on is the common spud or potato, if you prefer. Although we have saved it to last, it may very well be the best for it has some advantages over many other baits. First of all, the potato should be boiled until it is about half done. It can then be sliced or cubed to the proper hook size. One of the advantages to this bait is that it will stay on the hook until a carp comes along to take it. This is not true of the cereal and bread doughball baits that often desolve over a period of time or even nightcrawlers which frequently get nibbled away by other small fish.

One point to remember about baits, at least according to some experts, is that carp have a tendency to develop local preferences for certain foods. There are sections of some rivers where nightcrawlers are about the only thing that will take carp. There are reported lakes where the fishermen have educated the carp to accept only soaked sweet corn. And in one lake, they claim the carp turn their nose up at everything except a paste made of alfalfa and whiskey.

CHAPTER 8
ARTIFICIAL LURES

What will probably come as a surprise to many anglers is that carp can be taken on artificial lures. Obviously, the carp does not have much of a reputation for hitting lures. Few fishermen seek him in this manner but rather rely almost 100% on natural baits. It would be difficult to say exactly why because very little information has been written regarding this subject. It could be that carp only strike artificials on rare occasions. But on the other hand, it may be that the average fishermen simply doesn't know how to present his lure to entice the carp. More needs to be known regarding this subject.

It is a known fact that carp can be and have been caught on french spinners, bottom-running plugs and various flies on the surface. In almost every case, the angler was seeking some other fish when the lure was intercepted by a carp.

From what information is available, it appears that you must fish the lure extremely slow—repeat, extremely slow. The carp does not chase after a lure as many other fish will do. He likes to

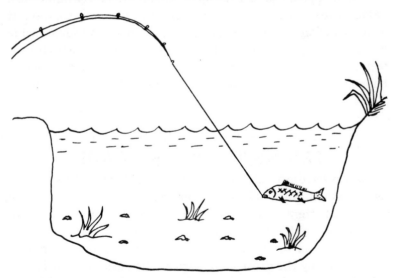

Pulling in a big stubborn fighting carp is a lot more fun than NOT pulling in a bass.

examine the bait before taking it in so it is essential that the lure move very, very slow.

There are two methods that have been known to take carp. It is an established fact that carp are mostly bottom-hugging scavengers. therefore, cast your lure and allow it to sink all the way to the bottom before starting your very slow bottom-bouncing retrieve. Because of the carp's exceptional keen sense of smell, you would probably increase your chances considerably by attaching a small piece of natural bait to the lure. Almost any of the tasty tidbits we listed in the chapter on baits would be effective.

One other method for taking carp on artificials, and probably the most exciting of all, is with your flyrod. During heavy insect hatches, or whenever you see carp scum skimming, they will readily take in artificial dry flies. If you ever tangle with a healthy chunk of carp under these conditions, you will find that it can be one of the most enduring and exciting battles a fisherman can get into.

There appears to be little questions that, slowly but surely, anglers are starting to pay a little more attention to Mr. Carp. It is my belief that it is only a question of time until some tackle manufacture or outdoor sports writer will come up with a lure or technique that Old Puckermouth will find to his liking. When it happens, and I hope it does, the fishermen will be better off for it.

CHAPTER 9
TRICKS THAT TAKE CARP

As we have already pointed out, carp have a very strong sense of smell. Although carp do not school such as bass, crappie or bluegill, they will on occasion gather in large groups to provide the angler with some fast and furious action. It is the strong smell of something good to eat that draws them to a certain spot by the droves. Sometimes the enticing odor is provided by mother nature, other times by some man made object or it can be deliberately set up by the fisherman which, in effect, makes the carp come to you.

Occasionally, you will find a lake or river with overhanging mulberry trees, wild grapes, red haws, etc., where the fruit tumbles down into the water. Carp love to congregate under these trees to feast on the wild fruit. Your best bet here is to simply place a piece of the fruit on your hook and toss it into the water where the other fruit is falling. No sinker or bobber would be necessary.

Good carp waters are within a short distance of almost every American. Most of our major cities were built on the banks of rivers that are today loaded with carp that are waiting to be caught.

Another excellent place to locate carp is below a dam or lock where fish get chopped up by the turbines used for generating electricity or by the opening and closing of the locks to allow boats and barges to pass.

Still another excellent place is around certain boat docks that maintain areas for fishermen to clean their catches. Often the remains of the cleaned fish; guts, liver, eggs, etc., are washed back into the water. It doesn't take the carp long to find these places and they will congregate by the dozens.

But perhaps the most popular method is for the fisherman to devise his own system of attracting the carp to his particular fishing spot. This can be done by a number of methods but they would all come under the heading called "chumming."

One method which we touched on previously is to toss in 2 or 3 handfulls of corn, the regular sweet kernels of corn from the can that you buy in any grocery store or supermarket. Other items could be corn meal, ground fish, chopped grain, cereal or you could simply pour in some liquid with a strong flavor such as beef bouillon soup, tobacco juice, fish oil, animal blood or immitation maple flavor. Any thing with a flavor that smells like something to eat is attractive to Old Man Carp.

One carp specialist uses nothing but fresh water clams. He will open several and leave them out until they take on a strong odor. Then he cuts them into little pieces and just before dark will go seed the area he plans to fish. The following morning he returns to that same spot and uses remaining pieces of the clams for bait and has a ball.

Still another method that accomplishes the same think is to take a loaf of bread, soak it in water, then work it with your hands until it becomes a thin gruel. Simply pour it onto the water to attract the carp. If you aren't in the mood to part with a loaf of bread, discarded scraps of sandwiches or the leftover breads would serve the same purpose.

While on the subject of bread, here are a couple of tricks you can try that will make your carp fishing immeasurably more exciting. Toss a few pieces of bread on the water. Insert your hook

Carp will congregate around anything that smells like a free meal, whether it is provided by nature or by the fisherman himself.

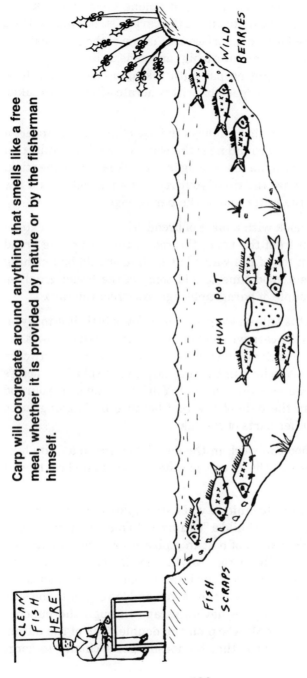

HOW TO MAKE A CHUM POT. Take a plastic carton or a milk carton, fill it with any kind of meat or vegetables, then punch holes in it to let the odors and flavors escape.

199

in a small piece of bread and flip it among them. No sinker or bobber. You are seeking to entice the carp to strike your surface bait. Nailing a bass on a surface bait is one of the angler's most exciting moments. Watching a big carp come up and suck in your breaded hook is right on par with taking a bass. You will be amazed at the rate of speed he will generate after he has taken your bait.

Another system that employs the use of bread is to insert a forked stick in the ground near the waters edge. Place your reel on the ground with the rod resting in the forked part of the stick. The idea is to have the tip of your rod remain steady just a few inches above the water and at the banks edge.

Bait your hook with a piece of bread. The line should extend straight down from the tip of the rod to the water. The bread should rest on top of the water but no line should be touching water. This is a good time to add some of the bread gruel we discussed a couple of paragraphs ago to attract the carp.

Now open the bale on your reel and allow a little line to lay on the ground so the carp will feel no resistance when he takes the bait. Then step back out of sight and wait. If there are any carp around, it won't be long until a big carp comes splashing across the top of the water to take the bait. You had better grab your rod quick and flip the bale of the reel because he is going to be heading for other parts of the lake.

This method can work in the day if you are on a quite lake but if there are any boats on the water, it is usually best to wait until night.

Still one other technique you can employ to attract carp to your fishing area is to build a "chum pot." This is extremely easy to do. Place some form of bait in a plastic or water proof paper carton such as a milk carton. Anything will work; cheese, vegetables, meats, etc., or any of the items listed in the chapter titled Baits. Punch some holes in the carton and lower it into the area you plan to fish. As the flavors escape through the punched holes, it will bring Mr. Carp on the double. One of the advantages to this system is that he doesn't get a chance to gorge himself on the bait such as he would on the food you would use for chumming. And all the time he is working up a fierce appetite as those odors keep escaping the carton. He will be ready for the taking when you drop in your baited hook.

It should be noted that some states do not allow chumming or the depositing of any such items in public waters. You should check your state laws.

A couple a final points. Carp often gorge themselves when food is plentiful. When they are full, they become inactive until the food is digested. This may account for occasional non-feeding periods.

We mentioned earlier that carp sometime start leaping for some unexplained reason. However, it has been noted they almost always start feeding shortly after the leaping period. So, when you see the carp leaping, get your line in the water, but quick.

And regardless of what time, when or where, always remember that carp are extremely wary fish. The slightest unnatural noise will send the carp scooting for deep water. Whether you are fishing from a boat or from shore, be absolutely as quite as possible.

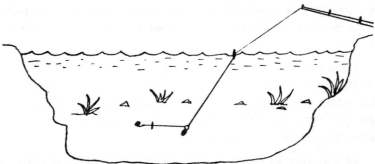

If you use a bobber, be sure it is very small. It is usually best to not use a sinker. If you do use one, be sure it is a slip sinker. A small stick 4 inches above the hook prevents sinker from sliding against bait. Carp are extremely wary. If they feel any resistance whatsoever, such as that of a sinker or bobber, they will drop the bait.

CHAPTER 10
BOW AND ARROW

If you find the art of taking carp by line and hook to be somewhat frustrating, there is another way to take them that is gaining in popularity with each passing year. It's not certain just how or when archers latched on to the carp but the only story around involves an Illinois gentleman that use to toss pieces of bread to a flock of ducks. Carp aren't all that dumb and it wasn't long until they were moving in to give the ducks a little competition. The gent happened to be a bow and arrow enthusiast and when he noticed the carp moving in each day when he started feeding the ducks, he soon developed some ideas of his own and perhaps this was the beginning of shooting carp with the bow and arrow.

At any rate, it requires no elaborate equipment. An adequate archery outfit can be purchased for a moderate price. It is best to use aluminum-tube arrows as they will float and can be retrieved. The barbs should be built for rugged handling and the arrowhead should be kept sharp. A reel is attached to the bow which allows the line to pull easily off the end. The line should be at least a 25 pound test.

If you are interested in this method of taking carp, your local sporting good store should be able to fix you up with an adequate archery outfit in addition to giving some pointers on how to use it.

Carp can be taken throughout the spring, summer and fall by bow and arrow. Spring is almost always best, especially during the spawning season. They can be seen in the shallows as they wallow about. During the summer, the evening hours are usually most productive.

To take carp by this method, you need to stalk them just as you would any other game. They can easily be spooked so it is essential that one always approach the area in the quietest manner possible. Once the arrow pierces the carp, he will fight just as hard as if he were on a baited hook. Archers frequently report of hand burns as a result of trying to slow a peeling line with a big carp on the other end.

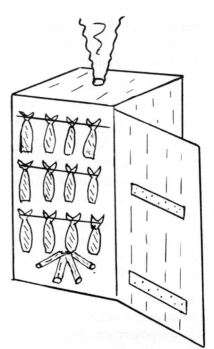

Smoked carp is a table delicacy that will draw raves from your friends.

This form of fishing may seem unsportsmanlike to some fishermen but it should be remembered that carp are prolific breeders and extremely hardy fish that will thrive and multiply in waters that will do other fish in. They can become over-abundant if not kept in check and it would seem that taking carp by bow and arrow would assist toward that end. It would certainy appear that archers present no serious threat to the carp's total population. However, this method is illegal in some states so again one should check.

CHAPTER 11
CARP RECIPES

There are many who claim that carp is not fit to eat. But there are also plenty of others who claim the carp taste just as good as any other fish in the world. The carp's bad reputation probably comes from the fact that he can and does inhabit dirty or polluted waters. But one should not judge a carp by his reputation. The only way you can know is to try him. We are listing on the following pages several recipes by which you can prepare the carp. Be sure to try a few of these. I can almost guarantee that you will find one or two of them to your liking and almost certainly they will be praised by your guests.

And by all means, try some smoked carp at your fist opportunity. Smoked carp is a table delicacy that will draw raves from your friends when served as hor d'oeuvres.

Carp can be french fried or pan fried just as you would most any other fish. First, roll the fillets in a beaten egg, then in a mixture of bread crumbs or corn meal. Add a dash of pepper and garlic salt and fry until done.

You may on occasion find a carp with a soft texture that will be lacking a satisfactory flavor. Don't discard it for it still has its full food value. Here is a mixture that will greatly enhance the flavor of the fillets.

1 cup salt   1 teaspoon pepper
1 large onion, minced   1/8 teaspoon mace
2 tablespoons vinegar

Mix the above ingredients in a deep bowl. Add the fish making certain that all parts are submerged. You might place a saucer over the fish to serve as a weight in accomplishing this. Allow the fish to stand in the mixture for one hour. Now discard the mixture, rinse the fish thoroughly and they are then ready to be cooked.

BROILED CARP

2 lbs. carp fillets   1/4 teaspoon pepper
3 tablespoons bacon drippings   1 medium sized onion
1/2 teaspoon salt   paprika

Rinse the fillets, wipe with a damp cloth, then place on rack of a broiler pan. Brush the top of the fillets with the bacon fat, season with the salt and pepper, then sprinkle with chopped onions and paprika. Place in a preheated broiler about two inches from the heat and broil for 5 minutes. Turn the fish over and repeat the same procedure with the other side. Broil another 5 minutes, or until done.

CARP AU GRATIN

Cut the carp fillets into small strips. In a skillet, fry 3 large chopped onions in butter until golden brown, then stir in one ounce of flour and remove from heat. Slowly add 1 pint of cream and stir as you re-heat. Add a dash of chopped parsley, nutmeg, sage, thyme, pepper, salt and mustard. Pour this over the fish, then sprinkle on a thick layer of grated cheese. Place in a hot oven for one hour and finish browning it under a grill if necessary.

PICKLED CARP

3 lbs. carp fillets	1/4 cup sugar
1 quart vinegar	1 teaspoon allspice
1 quart water	1 large onion, diced
1/3 cup salt	1/2 cup celery, chopped
1 teas. ground white pepper	

Mix all the above ingredients, except the carp, bring to a boil, then simmer for 20 minutes. Cut the carp fillets into strips about 3 inches long by 1/2 inch wide. Add them to the above mixture and let them simmer for an additional 15 minutes. Leave the fish in the pickling stock until it is cool. The pickled carp can be served as cold cuts or as appetizers.

The following 3 recipes are from Europe. All 3 are delicious and I strongly recommend that you try one or two of these at your first opportunity.

CARP IN BLACK SAUCE

2 tablespoons butter	1 tablespoon light brown sugar
1/3 cup diced celery	2 bay leaves
1/2 cup diced carrots	1/8 teaspoon thyme
1/2 cup diced parsnips	5 peppercorns
1/2 cup finely chopped onions	5 whole allspice
2 tablespoons sugar	2 slices lemon peel
1 teaspoon water	2 tablespoons red currant jelly
1 cup red wine	1/2 cup light beer
2 1/2 cups water	1/3 cup grated gingersnaps
1/3 cup pitted and chopped prunes	
1/4 cup chopped seedless raisins	
1 tablespoon slivered almonds	
A 4-lb. carp, cut into 6 eight ounce steaks, about 1 inch thick	

In a saucepan, melt the butter. Add the celery, carrots, parsnips and onions. Simmer for 10 minutes.

In another saucepan, mix the sugar with the water and cook for 3 minutes. Add the vinegar and bring to a boil. Add bay leaves, thyme, peppercorns, allspice, lemon peel, currant jelly and the steamed celery, carrots, parsnips and onions. Simmer over low heat for 1/2 hour. Add the beer, grated gingersnaps and brown sugar. Cook for another 5 minutes over medium heat or until sauce thickens slightly. Strain through a sieve, pressing down hard with a wooden spoon on the vegetables and condiments before discarding them.

Lightly butter a 4 quart casserole dish, arrange the carp steaks on the bottom. Pour the sauce over the carp, then sprinkle with chopped prunes, raisins, and slivered almonds. Bake the steaks in a 350 degree pre-heated oven for 10 to 15 minutes or until firm to touch, basting occasionally.

Serve the fish from the baking dish garnished with lemon wedges.

DALMATION STYLE CARP

3 pound carp cut into steaks about one inch thick.
Flour
4 tablespoons butter
2 tablespoons vegetable oil
1 pound onions, thinly sliced
1 pound tomatoes, chopped
1/2 cup dry white wine
1 tablespoon vinegar
1 teaspoon chopped tabasco peppers
1/4 teaspoon white pepper

Salt the fish steaks to taste, dip in flour and shake off the excess. In a skillet, heat half of the butter and oil, add the fish and cook for 2 1/2 minutes on each side or until lightly browned. Remove to a platter.

Heat the balance of the butter and oil in the skillet, add the onions and cook for 3 or 4 minutes. Add the tomatoes, wine vinegar, tabasco peppers and white pepper. Bring to a boil, stirring frequently. Return the fish to this mixture, tightly cover and simmer for 10 to 15 minutes. Place the fish on a platter and pour the sauce over them and serve.

DEVILED CARP

3 tablespoons bacon fat
1 cup finely chopped onions
2 tablespoons paprika
1 large green pepper diced
1 cup chopped tomatoes
1/4 cup dry white wine
5 pound carp cut into steaks about 1 inch thick.
Salt
Black Pepper
1/2 cup sour cream

Heat fat in a skillet and add the onions. Cook for 10 minutes. Stir in the paprika, then add the green pepper and tomatoes. Cover and cook for 5 minutes. Stir in the wine.

Place half of this mixutre into a buttered baking dish, add the fish steaks arranged in a layer in the baking dish. Salt and pepper the fish. Add the remaining vegetable mixture.

In a pre-heated 350 degree oven, bake the fish for 18 minutes, or until done. The fish should be firm to the touch and flake easily when prodded gently with a fork.

Remove the fish and arrange them on a serving platter. Cover them with foil and place the platter in a lowly heated oven to keep them warm while you prepare the sauce.

Make the sauce by whisking in a bowl 1/2 cup sour cream, 1/3 teaspoon salt, dash of black pepper, 1 tablespoon fresh lemon juice and 1 teaspoon paprika together. Place the sauce over a low heat, stirring constantly while it heats. Do not boil.

Season to taste. Pour the sauce over the fish and serve.

As we urged at the start of this chapter, don't knock the carp until you have tried it. Like thousands of other carp lovers, you just might like it. Try at least two of the preceding recipes. If the carp doesn't appeal to you in at least one of them, then he probably never will. I don't know whether the carp actually tastes different to different people or whether it is just a mental block that some people just can't seem to hurdle.

At any rate, Mr. Carp is here. He is here in abundance. All authorities agree that he's going to be here for a long time. There is really no justifiable reason why we should continue to ignore this fellow. So, why don't we recognize him for what he is, start giving him some attention and start having ourselves a lot of fun.

HOW TO SMOKE FISH
CHAPTER 1
INTRODUCTION TO SMOKE CURING

When I was a youngster, the sight of smoked fish didn't exactly turn me on. I can remember at our school educational movies seeing the smoked fish hanging in an Eskimo shack and they were simply not very attractive.

But I had never tasted any. That is, not until a few years ago.

One of my neighbors, a fellow named Larry, had just returned from a week-long fishing trip in Northern Michigan where he had caught a large quantity of Chinook Salmon. While there, he had several of the salmon smoked by one of the local residents, an Indian who had built himself a nice part-time business smoking fish. His fee was usually 50% of all the fish he smoked and his entire business investment consisted of a few bags of salt and a small wooden shed which he had built in his back yard.

Upon his return, Larry gave me one side of a smoked salmon with the challenge "try it, you'll like it."

I did and I was astonished. Having been born and raised in Kentucky, I always thought that a Country Cured Kentucky Ham was about the best eating a human would ever encounter.

But I had to admit, that smoked salmon was right on par with Country Cured Kentucky Ham. I've been a believer in smoked meat ever since. To the point, that I have since collected and read everything relating to the subject that I could find.

Apparently, smoke curing of meat goes back a long ways. Historians aren't really sure when it began. It is conceivable that even cave men might have enjoyed this delicacy. One thing is for certain. In the early days of our country, the pioneers had to have a food supply that would last through the cold winters until spring. Smoking and salt curing of meat was one of their chief ways of accomplishing this. It has been reported that frontiersmen such as Davy Crockett and Daniel Boone would go for days living on nothing more than buffalo jerky or smoked venison. It was made then pretty much as it is today.

Until recently, most smoking recipes were passed down from generation to generation by word-of-mouth and were adjusted by various persons to suit their own taste. But, regardless of where they got their recipes, it is an established fact that smoke flavored meat has been around for a long time. And its popularity shows no sign of decreasing. If anything, it's on the increase. One of the big drawbacks in recent years has been a lack of space for the big smokehouses such as our forefathers used. However, with the recent popularity of the condensed smokers, some of them no taller than 25 inches by 13 inches square, more and more people are taking up this delightful method of preparing food.

But the real beauty of it is that it is quite inexpensive. A well constructed wooden smoker will last a life-time and won't cost you but a few dollars. They can even be made from a cardboard box that will perform quite satisfactory. And, of course, they can be bought commercially. As of this writing, an electric heated, aluminum frame 25 inch by 14 inches square smoker can be bought for $40 some odd dollars.

It's always a satisfying feeling to turn out a product with that "just right" taste. However, unless one knows what he is doing, it could be a "hit and miss" proposition. The more you know about how smoking works, the better will be your chances for turning out a first class product with the right amount of flavor. The following information will assist you in achieving that end.

CHAPTER 2
SELECTING A SMOKER

There are about as many different designs of smokehouses as there are different styled automobiles. To many, there is the notion that a smokehouse is an elaborate construction that has to be built to certain specifications to obtain the desired results. Such is not the case. It can be a simple structure that will cost you less than $1.00. Ironically, the simple inexpensive smokers will turn out the same succulent products as the more elaborate ones.

There is also the notion that some mysterious formula has to be observed to turn out those mouth-watering morsels you have no doubt tasted from time to time. Again, not so. If you get too much salt or too little, smoke it an hour or so too long or too short or use any one of a dozen different types of wood, you haven't ruined the product. It will still be delicious. If you had done everything just right, it would no doubt have tasted better but this will come with experience. The point is — smoking fish and other meats is not difficult. By following simple instructions, the beginner can turn out delightful smoked flavored products on his very first try. With a little practice and experimenting with various spices and flavors, he can soon be the envy of his neighborhood. So let us proceed to build a smokehouse.

CHAPTER 3
CARDBOARD SMOKEHOUSE

By far the least expensive smokehouse you could build would be from a corrugated cardboard carton. Happily, it will do the same job that an expensive one will do. It would serve very well to smoke fish or game while on a prolonged camping trip. We would not recommend it as a permanent smoker since it just wouldn't be sturdy enough.

The size of the carton should be about 5 or 6 feet tall and 3 to 5 feet square. If you don't have a carton of this size, you could obtain one free from almost any hardware store, supermarket or any type of a retail store. They all throw them out by the dozens every day to be hauled away to the incinerator. If you could find one that a television set or refrigerator had been shipped in you would have one of about the right size.

The only tools needed are a sharp knife and a couple of other items, depending on which type box you construct. If you wish, you may take some wooden slats about one to two inches wide and glue them around the inside walls of the carton. These would be used as a support for the racks to hold the meat. In this case, you need four slats for each rack you intended to install plus a strong bonding glue.

Or, you could insert pieces of heavy gauge wire through both sides of the carton to form the rack. Coat hangers straightened with pliers and then cut to the proper length would serve the purpose quite well.

You will need to cut a small hole in the top for the smoke to escape. Also, cut a door in the bottom to attend the fire. You may want to use three or four small strips of tape to hold the top down while the meat is smoking. You should also bank a small mound of dirt around the bottom of the carton to prevent drafts from entering.

If you wish, you may use charcoal briquettes in an aluminum foil pan. Light the briquettes and when they begin to burn well, place the wood or chips or sawdust over the briquettes.

However, the briquettes are not necessary. You may build a small fire from the scraps of wood. Be sure to use hardwood such as hickory, oak, apple, alder or ash. Do not use pine, fir or any evergreen woods. These contain concentrates of creosote or resin and they will taint the fish.

Keep a close eye on the fire at all times. Do not allow it to blaze as it will get too hot. You only want it to smolder. You should keep a container of water close by to douse the flames if they get out of hand.

Also, the smoldering fire may get too hot. Check the meat occasionally. If it is fish you are smoking and they are dripping, you know it is too hot. You want them to cook very slowly so they will acquire that sweet, smoke flavor. It is not a bad idea to have a thermometer close by. The temperature in the top of the smoker should not exceed 180 degrees.

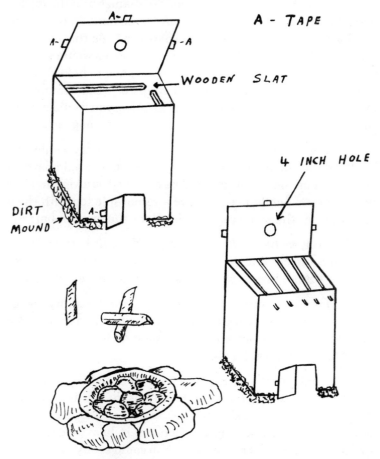

CARDBOARD SMOKERS
Two types of inexpensive cardboard smokers are illustrated. Top illustration has wooden slats to hold the rack. Bottom one has wires inserted thru the box to form the rack. If you wish, you may use charcoal briquettes. Place the hickory wood or chips on the charcoals to create the smoke.

CHAPTER 4
BARRELL SMOKERS

An old fashioned wooden barrell (if you can still find one) would make an excellent smoke house. You would need to have a removable top in order to insert and remove the meat. You would also need to drill a hole about 4 inches in diameter in the top for the smoke to escape. Racks would have to be built on the inside of the barrell to hold the meat. An easy way to do this would be attach two wire hooks to the inside top. The hooks would support a wooden rod to which nails would be inserted to hold the fish. Or, you could simply nail one inch strips of wood around the inside of the barrell to support the racks. Also, you would need to remove the bottom to allow the smoke to enter through a tunnel.

Perhaps an easier barrell type smoker for today would be a 50 or 100 gallon oil drum. Most every community would have an oil dealer where one of these could be obtained at a very modest cost. Again you would need to have a removable top with the 4 inch center for the same reasons listed for the wooden barrell.

However, we have two choices regarding the bottom. If you wish, you could cut out the bottom to allow the smoke to enter through a tunnel just as we outlined for the wooden barrell.

But for a more portable type smoker, and certainly just as effective, we could leave the bottom as is. Instead, we would cut a small door at the bottom side as we would do for the cardboard smoker to insert wood for the fire.

You would need to devise a method for installing the racks. Metal supports could be welded to the inside if you preferred. Perhaps an easier method would be to drill holes on each side of the barrell at the desired level, then insert heavy guage wire through the holes to form the racks. You could easily install two, three or four racks if you wished.

One thing about an oil drum smoker — it would be permanent. Take proper care of it and it would be around for many years.

CHAPTER 5
METAL SMOKERS

Any type of a box that will hold smoke can be converted into a very effective smoker. If you have a permanent outdoor grill, it can, with small modifications be adapted to serve as both a barbecue grill and a smoker.

Also, a portable barbecue grill can easily be adapted to serve as a smoker. It would need to be one of the larger grills but all that is needed is a top. Many grills come with a top and if you are planning to buy an outdoor grill in the future, I personally believe the ones with the enclosed tops for containing the smoke are by far the better buys. They cost a little more than the ones without the top but their extra versatility makes it a justifiable expense. Not only can they be used for the slow smoke process which we will describe later but barbecued steaks, pork chops, ribs, hot dogs, hamburgers, chickens, etc. all taste better when they take on the smoke flavor obtained from the enclosed type grills.

One other suggestion for a smoker is to use an old discarded refrigerator. These can be obtained from a junk dealer at an unbelievably low cost — from $1.00 up. Try to find one with the door in good operating condition and one with the racks still inside. Probably most would meet this requirement. Your only job now would be to get a hole through the top for the smoke to escape. If you preferred, you could install an electric heating unit of about 200 watts for smouldering the wood chips. Another choice would be to remove the bottom or you could just make a large hole in the bottom. It could then be placed over your outdoor grill or use the tunnel method which we will describe later.

It is usually best to avoid placing the grills too close to the top of the smoker. Since heat rises inside an enclosed structure, it usually gets quite a bit hotter near the top and could cause an uneven processing of the fish. The same may hold true if the meat is placed too near the fire.

CHAPTER 6
MANUFACTURED SMOKERS

In recent years, as our nation has experienced a revival in the art of smoking fish and meats, various companies have started to manufacture metal smokers. Although somewhat more expensive than building some of the smokers we have already described, they are nevertheless, quite compact and extremely convenient. For the fellow who is mostly all thumbs when it comes to building something, this may be a desirable solution.

One of the models that I am personally familiar with is called "The Little Chief". It is manufactured by Luhr Jensen and Sons, Inc. It is made of aluminum and its dimensions are 13 inches square by 25 inches high. It will hold up to 20 pounds of meat at a smoking.

It has an electric heating unit in the bottom consisting of a 115 volts AC. 170 watt U.L. approved element. All you do is plug in the heating unit and add the hickory chips (these come with the smoker) to the pan and within minutes the smoke is pouring out the top. It can be used on your patio or, since it only weighs a few pounds, can be taken on your camping trips if there is an electric outlet at the campsite.

CHAPTER 7
PERMANENT SMOKEHOUSES

There is no set rule for the dimensions of a smokehouse but for the fellow who does some occasional weekend fishing we would suggest the following as being the appropriate size for the average family — approximately 36 inches tall by about 18 inches square. Remember, that is only a suggestion. You may vary those dimensions any way you wish to suite your own need. It will not affect the ability of the smoker to perform its intended function.

It may be that you would have, somewhere around the house, an old wooden crate. With slight modifications, such as

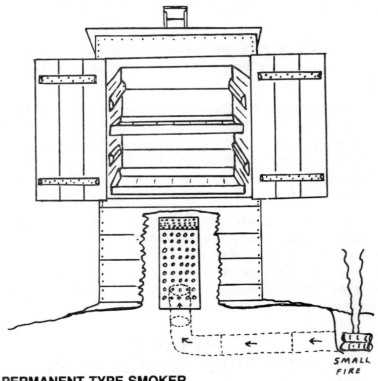

PERMANENT TYPE SMOKER
In this type smoker, the smoke is spread out by passing thru a
metal box or can which has many holes in it. Note the bend in
the underground pipe. The bend is important as it prevents the
sparks and ash from going directly into the smoker.

installing the racks, making a hinge door and removing the
floor; you are ready to go.

One final component to complete the smoker would be the
addition of a "smoke spreader." This is optional and not absolutely necessary but if a person is spending time and money to
build a good permanent smoker, he should probably go ahead
and include this item. It is nothing more than a can punched full
of holes installed beneath the smoker. As the smoke from the
stovepipe passes through the can, it would, to some degree,
spread the smoke out possibly eliminating hot spots and smoking the batch more evenly. Various items could be used for the

217

smoke spreader — a large bucket or a wooden box with holes, etc.

The bottom of your smoker should be of screen wire or else have an opening for the smoke to enter as it comes up through the flue.

We have described these as permanent smokers but there is no reason they could not be made into portables, if you wished, to be taken on extended fishing, hunting or camping trips. The portable part of your smoker would be the upper wooden box. This could be moved to set over an outdoor drill or over an underground flue.

If you are on a fishing or camping trip, a temporary underground flue can be built quite easily without a stovepipe. Simply dig a trench about a foot wide and a foot deep to possibly 3 to 6 feet long. Cover the trench with limbs or a board and then cover that with dirt. The smoker will, of course be placed over one end of the trench and the fire built at the other.

CHAPTER 8
COMMERCIAL SMOKEHOUSE

If you wanted to smoke fish or any other meats on a large scale, you can do so by simply constructing a large smokehouse. It is quite conceivable that a person could build himself a nice part-time or possibly full-time business in his backyard by building a commercial smoker. (Check your local ordinances first). A nice profit could perhaps be realized from smoked fish, smoked chickens, smoked hams, ribs or sausage, etc. Prospects would be delicatessen stores, restaurants, grocery stores or perhaps your own retail trade.

Sizes for such a smokehouse could range in the area of 45 to 50 inches square by about 84 inches tall. This is merely a suggestion. You may arrange the dimensions anyway you wish. In a smoker of this size, it would probably be best to retain the heating unit on the inside of the smoker thus eliminating the need for an underground flue. You could construct a concrete floor or simply have no floor and build your fire on the ground.

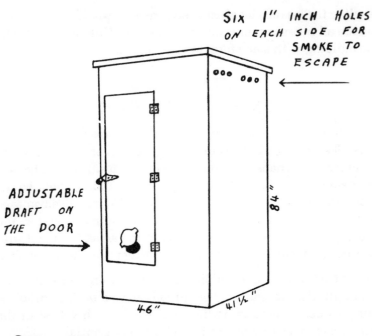

SIX 1" INCH HOLES ON EACH SIDE FOR SMOKE TO ESCAPE

ADJUSTABLE DRAFT ON THE DOOR

84"

46"

41½"

SUGGESTED SIZE
46 × 41½ × 84

COMMERCIAL SMOKEHOUSE

On this type smoker, the small fire should be built inside on the ground as this smoker has no floor. The interior walls should be covered with some form of sheet metal to lessen the chance of fire.

Without question, mother earth would serve the purpose as well as a concrete floor but it is quite possibly that your local health department would not allow you to sell food processed from such a structure. Any such ventures should always be cleared with the health department first.

In building a commercial smokehouse, simply incorporate the various features we have already described such as smoke racks, etc. One word of caution. In these larger smokehouses, you will obviously need a larger fire. This presents an element of risk inasmuch as the sparks could conceivably set your smoker on fire, which would not only destroy your smokehouse but could result in the loss of a lot of expensive meat. It would be advisable to take all necessary precautions to prevent this, such as lining the building with some form of sheet metal.

CHAPTER 9
INDOOR SMOKER

To my way of thinking, the indoor smoker would be the most desirable of all. Of course, it is nice to get outdoors in the summer, so perhaps we should consider two smokers. The outdoor smokers we have already described would no doubt be the least expensive. However, they have one distinct disadvantage — they are difficult, if not impossible, to use in the winter. You must maintain a low constant heat in the smoker and on wintery days this can be quite trying, not to mention the discomfort.

So let us consider building one inside your house. It is not that difficult, especially if you already have a built in fireplace with a flue. If there is no flue, you would be involved in the expense of installing one as this would be essential.

There would be two considerations. If you have the room, you might want to consider a permanent installation. It would be impractical at this point to try and describe a method for doing this inasmuch as it would have to be custom designed for the individual house. In designing such an installation, you would need to incorporate enough of the features of the outdoor models to do the job. It would be quite simple requiring only a small degree of imagination.

One word of caution. Since there will be considerable expense to installing a permanent indoor smoker, it would be wise to gain as much experience as possible with the less expensive outdoor models before proceeding. One of your primary considerations will be to determine the exact size that best suits your particular needs.

Of course, you don't have to make the indoor smoker a permanent installation. If you have a fireplace in your home, it may well be so designed that a box structure could be placed over the fireplace and then removed as desired. Simply follow the instructions for the outdoor smokers — an opening for the smoke to escape, racks for the meat. If the smoking unit is installed in the fireplace, you would need a box with the bottom removed so the smoke could pass up and through the box to surround the meat.

I would not want to consider a fire to generate the smoke. Sparks or excessive heat may ignite the box causing considerable damage to your home and perhaps completely destroying it.

However, a small electric heating unit of about 170 to 200 watts, properly installed, would be quite safe and do an excellent job. This would be enough heat to cause sawdust or wood chips to smoulder and that is exactly what you want.

CHAPTER 10
HOW SMOKE-CURING WORKS

Many people are under the impression that it is the smoke that cures the meat. Oddly enough, this isn't the case but rather, it is the heat that accompanies the smoke. As the smoke surrounds the meat, the heat is drawing out the moisture to preserve it while the smoke imparts its distinct flavor. It works this way. Air comes in at the bottom of the smoker. It passes over the smoldering wood to replace oxygen that has already been burned. It then moves up and around the meat carrying the smoke and heat with it as it seeks the escapement hole at the top of the smoker. Inasmuch as the smoke surrounds the meat, it is not necessary to turn the meat.

There are three basic ways to smoke food. Although similar in principal, they are each different and each needs to be understood to achieve the desired result.

First, we would classify as SMOKE COOKING. It is the hottest and fastest of the three methods. The temperatures using this method normally run in the neighborhood of 200 to 400 degrees. Probably, you have already practiced this method. It is no different than taking your backyard barbecue grill, putting a cover over it and cooking the meat by sprinkling hardwood chips over the charcoals.

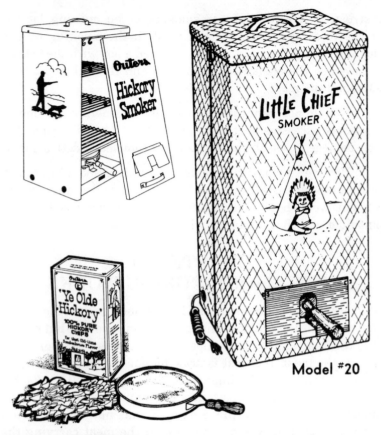

Model #20

ELECTRIC SMOKERS
These can be purchased from various sporting goods stores and mail order houses.

The second method we would call COLD SMOKING. In this method, the meat is placed on racks but somewhat distant from a low temperature smouldering fire. The meat is cured at approximately 90 degrees or lower for several days, even up to four weeks. This method is sometimes called Hard Smoking, depending on the length of preservation desired. The important factor in COLD SMOKING is that the temperature must not go over 90 degrees. You must keep the fire constant and low which means that someone has to be on hand at all times, even during the night, to maintain the proper level of heat. In the event the fire gets too hot, you will not get a properly cured product.

The third method and by far the most popular, is HOT SMOKING. In this method, you allow the temperature to range between 100 degrees to 190. You may allow the meat to cook entirely or partially, as you wish, as you impart the smoke flavor. With just a few ingredients and a simple, inexpensive, home-made smoker; you can turn out mouth-watering smoke fish, turkey, hams, cheese, old fashioned jerky, oysters, bacon, hot dogs, spareribs, sausage, hors d'oeures and many, many other foods with a gourmet flavor that no commercial meat packer could afford to attempt.

CHAPTER 11
CURING PROCEDURE

Before attempting to smoke meat or fish, there is another curing process that must be observed. Remember, the smoke only imparts the flavor. It is these other processes that effect the preservation of the meat. There are two curing methods that may be used prior to putting the meat in the smoker. These are the DRY CURE method and BRINE CURE method. These are simply mixtures of salt, sugar and spices.

In the DRY CURE method, you simply rub the salt mixture onto the meat. In the BRINE CURE, you put the salt mixture into water to form a brine, then soak the meat in the brine solution. They both accomplish the same goal. About the only difference is that the DRY CURE will normally produce a "saltier" flavor and usually causes more shrinkage than the BRINE method.

Here's how it works. Meat fermentation or spoilage is caused by micro-organisms. The micro-organisms need water to flourish. The function of the salt is that it draws the water out of the meat making spoilage conditions much more difficult. This is why salt is put in butter — to keep it from spoiling. Even fresh caught fish, immediately upon cleaning, should be put in a salt water solution — again to prevent spoilage. Now, after proper salt curing (your recipes will tell you how long), the meat should be dried for a short interval, then it is ready for the smoker where the heat removes the remaining moisture to effect the final cure.

No matter what foods you are attempting to prepare, it is always a good rule of thumb to buy the best ingredients possible. It is usually best to buy a pre-mixed curing salt that is available at most farm stores and some grocery stores or butcher shops. One of the better ones is Morton's Sugar Cure Salt. It is a smoke flavored, home meat curing salt. If no curing salt is available, your next best bet is a course salt going under trade name such as Ever-Soft and Sof-T-Soft. These can usually be bought in 10 lb., 25 lb., or 100 lb. bags. Be sure that it is a pure salt. The pure salt has fewer chemical impurities which may delay penetration. Salts containing impurities, such as rock salt, may give the meat a bitter taste. If necessary, you can use regular table salt but the pre-mixes are more desirable.

Again, referring to the DRY CURE and the BRINE CURE, each has its own place in preparing meat for the smoker. We will include several recipes later and they will list which cure is more desirable. The Dry Cure is faster but as previously mentioned it may cause the meat to shrink and often has a saltier flavor. Normally, you simply rub the salt mixture on the meat and let it stand for the alloted time before putting it in the smoker. **IMPORTANT NOTE!** Always remember to wash off the meat and let it air dry before placing it in the smoker.

When you Brine Cure prior to smoking, the meat will usually show less shrinkage, it will be a little more moist and it normally appears to retain somewhat more flavor than the Dry Cure. If you Brine Cure, be sure to use a container that is made from glass, plastic or enamel. An excellent choice in the old time 5 or 10 gallon stoneware crock. I remember that my mother use to brine cure pickles in such a crock and they were delicious. (It is also useful for making home brew if you happen to be such an enthusiast). The stoneware has a tendency not to absorb foreign flavors into the container walls as some other materials might do.

Do not use metal containers for the brine cure, especially aluminum. Salt causes metal to become very corrosive and will often cause the meat to discolor and take on a bitter metallic taste.

When brine curing, be sure to make enough solution to submerge the meat entirely. Some sort of a weight, such as a plate or saucer, should be used to keep the meat completely under the surface. If any portion of the meat extends above the solution into the open air, there is an excellent possibility that spoilage will occur.

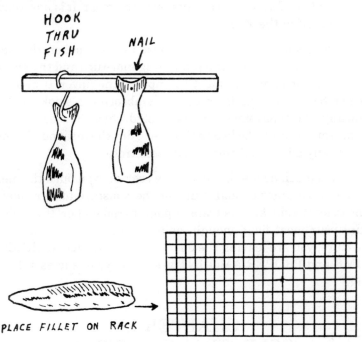

Three methods for placing fish or meat in the smoker. You may obtain some excellent racks from old discarded stoves and refrigerators.

Once you have accumulated some experience, you may wish to vary the amount of salt, sugar and spices to suit your own taste. After you have left the meat in the brine solution for the required amount of time, remove it and then ALWAYS rinse it off under cold running water. You should then allow the meat to dry at normal room temperature for approximately one hour.

225

Should you omit the WASH and DRY part of the procedure, you will notice that after the meat is placed in the smoker, it will sweat, creating a black condensation on the inside top of your smoker. This condensation then drips back on the meat creating a sour taste. It is not a bad idea to take a dry paper towel and gently press it to the meat to absorb as much of the moisture as possible before this one-hour drying period starts. You will notice that at the end of the drying period, there will be a tacky glaze that has formed on the outside of the meat. It is now ready to be placed in the smoker.

Once you have placed the meat in the smoker, the heat starts to slowly remove the remaining moisture and the smoke begins to penetrate the meat to improve the flavor. It must be remembered that the meat can only absorb the smoke so fast and any additional smoke will be wasted. Once the meat reaches a saturation point, the heat will have to dry the meat out further before any additional smoke will penetrate.

Too much heat will too quickly cook or even burn the meat and will not allow enough time for the moisture to be removed and to let the smoke penetrate. A point to remember! If you don't cure your meat long enough, or if you don't use enough salt mixture, you are leaving the door open for spoilage. CORRECT TIME and PROPER AMOUNT are the keys to successful curing.

CHAPTER 12
SELECTING THE WOOD

The type of wood you choose to smoke your meat is dependent upon the individuals taste. Different woods obviously produce different smoke flavors. A few of the more popular woods that are used for smoking are hickory, birch, oak or maple. Also, such items as driftwood, grape vine trimmings, tree leaves, corn cobs, green wood and seaweed. Almost without question, the old fashioned kiln dried hickory flavor is the most popular.

Hickory sawdust is perhaps the ideal smoker fuel for it smolders slowly and evenly and creates a thick smoke. In the olden days, it was quite widespread to use wet or damp sawdust or sometimes green wood in an effort to control the temperature. However, this required constant attention for if the pile of sawdust over the coals dried out it would start to burn and raise the temperature too high.

This is one of the advantages of the electric commercials smokers which we previously mentioned. The heating element in these smokers remain constant and at just the right temperature for maintaining maximum smoke production and penetration. Also, there is little chance that it will get too hot which eliminates the fear of burning the meat. In some items, such as jerky, which you would want to smoke slowly for eight hours, the controlled temperatures of the commercial smokers greatly improve your chances of success. If you wish, you could add chunks of hickory to the sawdust to produce a longer and slower smoke. You may also want to experiment with different woods and mix them with the hickory dust to produce a flavor particularly pleasing to your own taste. You want to avoid such woods as pine, fir or hemlock as they sometimes give the meat a bitter coal tar or creosote flavor.

CHAPTER 13
HOW TO SMOKE FISH

Here is a method for smoking fish that will produce mouth watering morsels time after time.

First, make a brine mix. Be sure to follow previous instructions regarding the type of container. Mix these ingredients together. From here on we will refer to this as the Standard Brine Mix.

STANDARD BRINE MIX

1 quart of water	**½ cup sugar**
½ cup salt	**Seasoning to taste**

This quantity is about right for 10 pounds of fish, or less. If you have a larger amount of fish, you would need to increase the above quantity accordingly.

Place the fillets or chunks of fish skin side up in the brine. Be absolute certain that all portions of the meat is submerged in the brine. It would be well to cover the fish with a large dinner plate making sure the plate is just below the brine surface.

Leave the fish in the brine solution for at least five hours. If you prefer a saltier flavor leave them six hours. After the five or six hours has elapsed, take the fish out of the brine solution, rinse each piece and as you do so, gently rub the meat until the slippery feeling from the brine solution is washed off.

Now spread the fish out on a paper towel with the skin side down. With another paper towel, absorb as much of the moisture from the fish as possible. Then leave the fish to air dry for 60 minutes. You'll know when the air drying is completed because the fish develop a tacky glaze on the outside. While the fish are air drying, it would be well to get your smoker started. If you have it adequately preheated, the fish will start the smoke cure the moment you put them in the smoker.

As soon as the air drying is completed, your fish are ready to be placed on the smoker racks. If you desire additional seasoning such as onion, garlic, brown sugar or maple flavoring; now is the time to rub it in. As you arrange the meat on the smoker racks, place the skin side down making certain that the pieces are not touching each other. If they touch, they have a tendency to become glued to each other. Also, you should make certain there is space between the fish to allow the smoke to better surround the meat.

You should put the thickest chunks or fillets on the bottom rack and the thinner ones near the center and up. The bottom ones, being closer to the heat, will complete the curing faster. It is unnecessary to turn the fish after they have been placed on the rack.

You will need to give some consideration to the location of the smoker. If it is located in a windy or drafty area, there will be a chill factor to consider. It would be best if you could locate the smoker in a sheltered area if the weather is very windy or cold.

It will be necessary that you make frequent checks to make

certain that your smoker doesn't get too hot. Remember, the meat can reach a saturation point as it will only accept so much smoke at a certain rate. You will also need to occasionally add more sawdust or wood chips in order to maintain a constant and steady temperature in addition to keeping a dense smoke.

Some recipes may suggest that the smoking fuel be damped, but this is a highly questionable practice. This will simply transfer the moiture into the smoker and onto the meat. This defeats what you are trying to do. Your main object is to remove the moisture from the meat so it would be best that you not dampen the smoking fuel.

You should begin to check the fish for doneness after they have been in the smoker for about six hours. From that point on, you should check at least every half hour. There are some signs you can look for to tell when the fish are ready to remove from the smoker. At first, the meat will start to turn a pale grayish color. Then, as it becomes done, it will begin to darken and get firmer.

When the fish are completely done, the outside will take on a bronze glazed appearance similar to the outside of a roast turkey. However, you can't rely on color alone as different species of fish will take on different colors. It would be more reliable to gently break open a couple of pieces to check and see if they are done in the center. When they are done, the meat should flake apart easily. The thinner chunks or fillets will usually get done before the thicker ones so they should be removed first and then finish up the thicker ones.

After the smoked fish are taken from the smoker, they should be allowed to cool at room temperature for a half an hour. The pieces should then be put in air tight containers and placed in the refrigerator for one to two hours before serving.

If you wish, you can spruce up the appearance of the smoked fish by brushing the pieces with corn oil, vegetable oil, cottonseed oil, soya oil or with melted butter. This should be done while the fish are still warm.

You have probably seen smoked fish at the local meat

market that were a vivid red. This is because they were commerically produced and then dyed an artificial reddish-orange for consumer sales appeal. The natural color of the Chinook and Sockeye salmon is a reddish orange and this seems to be the

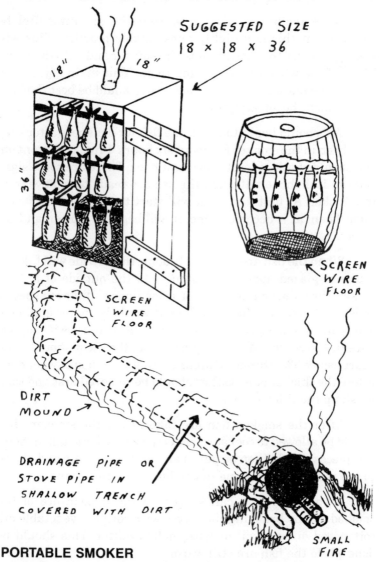

SUGGESTED SIZE
18 × 18 × 36

18"   18"

36"

SCREEN WIRE FLOOR

SCREEN WIRE FLOOR

DIRT MOUND

DRAINAGE PIPE OR STOVE PIPE IN SHALLOW TRENCH COVERED WITH DIRT

SMALL FIRE

PORTABLE SMOKER
A popular type smoker for the backyard or camp site. A simple old-fashioned barrel would serve the same purpose.

230

ultimate goal for most producers of commercially produced smoked fish regardless of which species they are smoking.

So if your home-smoked fish don't have that vivid red appearance, don't be disappointed. It isn't supposed to. However, if you wish to color your smoked fish, it is quite easy to do so. Get some red and orange food dye, make a mixture of ¼ ounce red, ¼ ounce orange in two gallons of water. Dip your fish in this mixture for approximately a half a minute after rinsing off the brine and just prior to the air drying process.

To obtain variations in the flavor, try adding various spices. These are often added directly to the brine but if you want a more distinct taste, you may rub the spice onto the meat just after you have rinsed the brine from the fish and again, just prior to the air drying. It would be best if you experimented with various spices until you obtain the flavor cure you think best.

Here are some spices or flavors that you might try experimenting with: brown sugar, onion salt, tabasco sauce, white pepper, mace, garlic, dill, molasses, lemon juice, honey, ginger, bay leaves, all spice, maple flavoring, soy sauce — just to name a few.

In fact, if you want to become an instant hit with your neighbors or fishing buddies, try this following recipe.

1 quart water — 2 cups of brown sugar — 2 cups of salt

Then take any one of the above spices and add just enough to give it the flavor you want.

OUT OF SIGHT!

CHAPTER 14
PRESERVATION OF FISH
AND MEAT IN THE FIELD

In order for the outdoorsman to end up with a high quality smoked product, it is absolutely essential that he start out with a fish or piece of meat that has experienced no spoilage. This can be difficult unless proper attention is given to the fish or game at the time it is taken.

You have, perhaps, at one time or another prepared a mess of bluegill or some other panfish in which most of the pieces tasted fresh and delicious but an occasional piece would have that "fishy" taste. What probably happened is that the ones with the off taste had been caught early in the day and by the time the fisherman got home that evening to clean the fish, it had already started to deteriorate. This could have been avoided if proper precautions had been taken when the fish was first caught.

The same can be said of most game. You have probably heard of some people who can't stand the taste of deer meat. They claim it has a sour or a funny flavor. The odds are that something probably happened to taint the meat, for most experts agree that deer meat, properly field dressed, stored, cooled and prepared will provide a meal that is out of this world. The same can be said of most wild game.

Fishermen especially have a tough battle to fight against spoilage, since fish, unless properly cared for, will start to deteriorate rather quickly. If you catch any fish early of a morning and are not planning to return until that evening, you would do well, especially on hot days, to take time out for some protective measures. (As a person who loves to fish, I know that this can be down right frustrating if the fish are biting.)

You should at least cut the gills out and bleed them. Also, gut it to remove all internal organs from the belly cavity. If it is going to be a long time before you get to a cooler or refrigerator, you should rub the belly cavity with salt and cover the fish with wet burlap or leaves and keep them in a shady spot. When kept this way, the fish should be good for 24 hours without ice.

In fact, when commercial salmon trollers in the Pacific make a catch, proper dressing is immediately given top priority. They dress the salmon thoroughly, making certain the cavity is absolutely clean before icing the fish down to go in the hold. Often, it will be seven days before they will head to port so the fish have to stay fresh for a long time.

The important thing to remember is that even the smallest portion of blood or membrance that is left in the cavity becomes a prime area for deterioration to start. Warmth and moisture are the primary ingredients in which micro-organisms thrive to cause spoilage. The ideal temperature for them to work in is between 70 and 100 degrees F. The best temperatures for storing fresh meat for maximum preservation is between 33 to 40 degrees F. At least, this is the temperatures preferred by most meat cutters. The important thing to remember is that the way you care for your fish or game can make a tremendous difference in the way it will taste when it reaches the table.

CHAPTER 15
SMOKING FROZEN FISH

As we have already mentioned, some attention should be given to fish shortly after they are caught if it is going to be a lengthy period before they are cleaned. They should be gutted and bled and kept in a moist shady place if possible. The sooner the fish can be cured or frozen, the better are your chances for a tasty product and the less chance of spoilage.

Let's give some attention to the freezing of fish. For in a moment I want to tell you of how to devise a freezing and smoking system that will put delicious morsels of smoked fish at your fingertips any day of the year. I will mention here that frozen fish, when properly thawed, are excellent for smoking. In fact, the freezing appears to open up the cells to accept the smoke better.

If fish are not properly prepared for the freezer, they cannot be expected to last too long. If any air reaches portions of the fish while they are in the freezer, there is an excellent chance of "freezer burn" which is a combination of dehydration and oxidation. There are three methods that if properly observed, will prevent freezer burn. (1) Double wrap the fish in a moisture proof material, such as saran wrap, being sure to squeeze out all the air, (2) in an air-tight container, such as plastic freezer containers or (3) glazing, which is freezing the fish in a container of water.

If you clean your fish before you freeze them (and it's quite acceptable if you do), you should do so as soon as possible after the catch. Each hour you delay can effect the taste. However, here is a system that I personally think is better.

In an earlier chapter, I described how you can take your fish whole, no scaling, no cleaning whatsoever; put them in a plastic bag and freeze them. I also described what I thought was even a better way, to place the whole freshly caught fish in a plastic container, fill it with water and freeze the entire fish in ice.

Either way is fine. The point is you don't clean the fish until you remove it from the freezer, perhaps four to six months later and then clean it after it thaws out.

After thawing, the fish are ready for brine curing and then the smoke curing process.

You should also observe certain procedures for thawing the fish in order to obtain best results. They should be thawed slowly as this tends to keep the flesh firm. Fish that have been frozen in air-tight containers should be placed in a refrigerator at 37 to 40 degrees F. and allowed to slowly thaw at these temperatures. Fish that were frozen in water could be placed under running cold tap water to gradually thaw.

If there is any question as to whether or not the fish has spoiled, gently press down on the skin with your finger. If the flesh springs back, it indicates that it should be OK. However, if a dent remains, it suggests a borderline case which could be spoiled.

A moment ago, I mentioned that I would suggest a method that would save you considerable time and keep various smoked gourmet goodies at your fingertips most of the year and here it is.

If your fishing trips are like mine, you perhaps do better on some days than others. There have been more times than I like to remember when I have returned home with scarcely enough fish to make them worth while to clean. Also, (I hate to admit it) but as the years keep slipping by, I've noticed that when I get home after a day on the lake, I'm not always too terribly energetic when it comes time to clean the fish.

In fact, here of late, they don't get cleaned. I simply toss them in a plastic container, fill it with water to totally cover the fish, then into the freezer. After four or five such trips (by this time the wife starts screaming there's no room in the freezer), I take them out and clean them all at once. Then we're set for a big

Above illustration shows how a backyard smoker can easily be made from a discarded 50 gallon oil drum. Old discarded refrigerators can easily be made into excellent smokers.

fish fry with fish as fresh as the day they were caught. Or, I sometimes hook up the smoker but instead of smoking just four or five pounds as I might have after a single fishing trip, I am now smoking fifteen to twenty pounds which makes it a lot more worth while. It requires no more time, expense or effort to smoke twenty pounds of meat than it does to smoke one pound. And this way, you can store up smoked goodies for year-round eating.

Here are a couple of facts you should note and remember.

(1) Smoked fish kept in the refrigerator will last about two weeks.

(2) Smoked fish kept in the freezer will last at least a full year. When wrapping for the freezer, they should be packed in usable portions. Once the frozen package is thawed, the fish should be eaten within a reasonable time and not refrozen.

Normally, when we think of smoked fish, the thought of smoked salmon or herring comes to mind. But we shouldn't limit ourselves to just these two fish. Most all fish are easy to smoke — catfish, bass, carp, trout and many others. Try experimenting with the more popular fish in your area. Use different smoke flavors to see what you can come up with.

CHAPTER 16
DUTCH SMOKED FISH

The Dutch have devised a method for preserving smoked fish that will keep them eatable for a considerable period of time. After the fish have been taken from the smoker, cut them into small pieces. Remove all pieces of skin and pack the chunks of fish in small jars or home canning jars. Finish filling the jar with vegetable oil until the fish are covered. Then seal and store the jars in a cool place until ready for use.

The jars and caps should be thoroughly scalded prior to filling. It would be much safer if you used the home canning lids that can be purchased at most any supermarket or grocery store. There are three companies I am aware of that manufacture these lids — Bernardin, Kerr and Ball. They are all equal in quality and function in the same manner.

The oil should be poured in hot and the lid should be screwed on immediately. As the oil starts to cool, you will hear a "snap" and, if you will note, after the snap the center of the cap will have sunken. This means you have "drawn a vacuum", assuring you of a safe pack as long as the center of the cap remains sunken.

CHAPTER 17
HOW TO SMOKE CARP

Many people contend that a carp is not fit to eat but if you will prepare one in the following manner, I believe you will be pleasantly surprised. A properly smoked carp is downright good eating.

First, the fish should be skinned. All traces of the skin and scales should be removed. This can be accomplished in a number of ways. There are skin removers that can be bought which will do the job nicely. Or, a good sharp knife will do the same job.

There are two methods you can follow using a knife. One, hold the fish by the tail and slip the knife blade beneath the skin as close to the tail as possible. In a sawing motion, start cutting toward the head removing a narrow strip of skin as you go. About three passes on each side should have the skin removed.

This leaves the white clean meat exposed. Now fillet the fish. First, make a deep cut all the way to the bone along the top side from head to tail. Now start just behind the gills and cut toward the tail. As you cut, keep your knife blade pressed against the rib cage. You want to remove as much of the side meat as possible in one piece. When you have finished, you should have two side slabs of white meat. Throw the carcass away.

Another method is to fillet the fish before cleaning. This would be more or less a matter of reversing the above procedure. Take the fish while he is still whole (no need to remove the scales) and make a slice along the top side from head to tail. Cut deep all the way to the backbone on either side of the dorsal fin. Then insert the knife blade just behind the gills. Cut toward the tail keeping as close to the rib cage as possible to remove the fillets from each side. Discard the carcass.

Now take the fillets and place them, skin down, on a board. With your thumb, hold one corner of the skin to the board. Insert the knife blade between the skin and the meat and separate them by sliding the blade along the board. Skin and scales are removed at the same time.

Wash the fillet and place in the standard fish brine solution. Follow the normal procedure from here on as outlined in the chapter on How To Smoke Fish.

CHAPTER 18
RECIPES FOR SMOKED FISH

This book has been primarily concerned with the "Hot Smoke Method" of smoking fish and other items. With this method, there is nothing further that needs to be done. The meat is ready to eat as soon as the smoking is completed and it will be delicious down to the last bite.

However, for a little variety, there are other ways the fish can be prepared after the smoking process is completed. For some out-of-this-world eating, I strongly recommend that you try one or two of the following recipes at your first opportunity. These are dishes you will probably never find in any restaurant.

BAKED SMOKED FISH

Take the smoked fish and freshen it in cold water for one hour or more before cooking. Dry and place the fish in a greased baking dish, flesh side up. Brush with cooking oil or butter, then sprinkle with finely diced onion and carrot. Cover the fish with milk and bake from 20 minutes to 1 hour, according to thickness of fish. Baste from time to time as the milk evaporates. Remove when done and garnish with parsley.

SMOKED FISHBURGERS

2 cups flaked fish (either leftover or canned)
2 eggs (beaten)
1 cup crackers or bread crumbs
1 tablespoon minced onion
salt and pepper to taste

Place the flaked fish in a greased baking dish spreading it even over bottom of dish. Set dish uncovered in the smoker for one hour. Remove and allow to cool, then add the fish to the remaining ingredients, mixing thoroughly. Shape into patties and fry in hot grease or hot butter until golden brown. Can be eaten as a sandwich or served on toast with white sauce.

SMOKED FISH AND SCALLOPED POTATOES

2 cups of smoked flaked fish
4 tablespoons bacon fat
4 tablespoons flour
2 teaspoons lemon juice
1 cup milk
1 cup of smoked fish stock
2 cups of sliced cooked potatoes (boiled)
1 teaspoon tobasco sauce
salt and pepper to taste

In a bowl, mix the bacon fat, flour, lemon juice, tobasco sauce, salt and pepper. Stir in the milk and fish stock to make a cream sauce. In a greased casserole dish, place a layer of potatoes, a layer of fish then cover with sauce, another layer of potatoes, fish, sauce, etc. until the ingredients are exhausted. Baked until piping hot and nicely browned.

SMOKED FISH SOUFFLE

2 eggs, separate the yolks and whites
2 cups of cooked rice
1½ cups milk
1 cup of smoked fish (flaked)
2 tablespoons bacon fat or butter
Add salt, pepper and paprika to taste

Beat the egg yolks thoroughly. Add all the remaining items except the egg whites. In a separate bowl, beat the egg whites until stiff. Now blend in the egg yolks mixture with the stiff egg whites. Pour into a greased baking dish and bake for 45 minutes at 350 degrees. May be served with or without a fish sauce.

SMOKED FISH CROQUETTES

2 eggs
2 cups of flaked smoked fish
1 cup of mashed potatoes
Salt and pepper to taste
Dash of garlic powder (optional)
Bread crumbs and milk

Beat one egg thoroughly. Add the fish flakes, potatoes, salt and pepper. Mix well, then form into croquettes. Roll the croquettes in the bread crumbs.

In a separate bowl, beat the other egg and add a little milk. Dip the croquettes into the beaten egg, then roll in the bread crumbs again. Deep fry at 390 degrees until golden brown. Serve hot.

CREAMED SMOKED FISH

1½ cups of flaked smoked fish
1 cup milk
1 cup fish stock
4 tablespoons flour
4 tablespoons bacon fat
1 teaspoon Worchestershire Sauce
Salt and pepper to taste

Mix the flour, bacon fat, salt and pepper. Add the milk and fish stock and stir into a smooth white sauce. Add the fish flakes, heat until piping hot, then serve. For variety, carrots, peas, eggs, parsley, etc., may be added.

SMOKED CANNED SALMON OR TUNA

How about a smoke-flavored sandwich. This one is hard to beat. Take a can of salmon or tuna, drain the liquid and then place the meat on a greased baking dish — one that wll fit inside your smoker. Spread the fish out over the dish by flaking it with a fork. Now place it in the smoker and smoke for about one hour. Then remove, allow to cool and it is ready to be prepared into your favorite sandwich spread — one with a smoked flavored fish taste. I can assure you that it will be delicious.

SMOKED OYSTERS

If you want a morsel fit for a king, sample this one at your first opportunity. Prior to brine cure, the oysters should be blanched. This is easy. Place the oysters in a metal strainer and dip them into boiling water for two or three minutes. Remove them when the edges start to cure, then rinse under cool tap water.

241

Now place the oysters in a standard fish brine for 40 minutes. Give them a 45 minute air dry, then on to an oiled screen and into the smoker for 50 to 75 minutes. Be careful that you don't overcook as they will become quite tough. They are starting to get done when the edges begin to look dried out but if in doubt, take one out and taste it.

SMOKED CLAMS

Clams should be cured in a standard fish brine for 20 to 30 minutes. Allow to air dry for 40 minutes, then onto an oiled screen and into the smoker for 2 to 2½ hours.

SMOKED SMELT

Prepare smelt by removing head and guts. Cure in a standard fish brine for 1½ hours. Air dry for 45 minutes. Smelt should be smoked for three to four hours.

SMOKED HERRING

Only fresh herring should be smoked. Cure in a standard fish brine for 30 to 45 minutes. Rinse and air dry for 60 minutes. Herring should be smoked from two to three hours.

SMOKED SHRIMP and CRAYFISH

These should be precooked prior to brine cure. If uncooked, place in boiling water for five minutes. Now put the meat into a standard fish brine for two hours, then rinse and dry excessive moisture with paper towels. Allow them to air dry, then place on an oiled screen on the smoker racks and smoke them for about 1½ hours. The shrimp should be arranged on the screen so they are not touching.

CHAPTER 19
ADDITIONAL RECIPES
OR
HOW TO WIN FRIENDS
AND INFLUENCE PEOPLE

I hope Dale Carnegie doesn't mind me using the title to his book as a sub-title for this chapter, but if you have a desire to impress your friends and make new ones, try serving them with a few of the following treats.

STEAKS OR CHOPS

About one hour before you would normally start preparing your steak or chops, put them in your smoker. After one hour in the smoker, take the meat and prepare it by your best method. They will take on an unbelievable flavor that will draw raves from your friends. Be sure to try this one.

SMOKED TURKEY OR GOOSE

Like most fowl, smoked turkey or goose makes a scrumptious meal. In preparing any fowl for smoking, whether turkey, chicken, duck, etc.; it should always be the freshest one you can obtain. If the turkey is frozen, it should be thawed per the instructions on the label. Below is the brine mixture for turkey.

4 quarts of water	½ cup lemon juice
1½ cups of curing salt	½ ounce maple flavoring
½ cup brown sugar	½ teaspoon ginger
3 cups cider	4 tablespoons black pepper

The brine mixture should be in a large container, non-aluminum, big enough to completely submerge the entire turkey. You should then simmer over a medium heat — five minutes for each pound of meat.

Take the bird from the brine and air dry for one hour. After the air dry, rub the skin with brown sugar, then suspend it from a bar across the smoker. A drip pan can be made on the bottom rack from aluminum foil.

Baste each 1½ hours with melted butter. Leave turkey in the smoker for one hour for each pound of meat. Then remove from smoker and place in a roasting oven preheated to 300 degrees. When done, the big joint will move easily in the socket. Turkey cooked in this manner will last about as long as a normally roasted turkey. If you wish to put the leftovers in the freezer, they will keep about seven months.

SMOKED: Chicken, Pheasant, Quail Duck, Ptarmigan, Grouse

Smoked fowl, whether it's pen raised chicken or wild pheasant, duck, quail, etc., is a superb dish. The fowl should be fresh and it can be smoked whole, halved or cut into pieces. If frozen, leave in the refrigerator until completely thawed. The following is the brine formula for each.

2 quarts of water	4 tablespoons black pepper
1 cup curing salt	¼ cup lemon juice
½ cup brown sugar	¼ teaspoon maple flavoring
1 tablespoon onion powder	1 bay leaf

Let the fowl brine-cure for one hour for each pound of meat. Make certain that all portions are immersed in the brine by placing weighted plate over the meat.

After the brine cure is complete, remove, rinse under cold tap water, wipe off the excessive moisture then allow to air dry for one hour.

244

After the air dry, rub the below mixture into the meat.

½ cup brown sugar
1 tablespoon garlic powder or onion powder
4 tablespoons black pepper

Now place fowl in the smoker. If the bird is whole, it should be suspended from a bar across the smoker. If bird is cut up, just place the parts on the smoker racks. You should smoke the fowl for 1½ hours for each pound of meat. If you wish, you might place a sheet of aluminum foil on a lower rack under the bird to catch the drippings. Every 1½ hours, you should brush the fowl with butter. For extra flavor, you might add other sauces to the butter, such as barbecue sauce or beer.

You can tell when the fowl is done by gently twisting the leg bone. If it moves easily in the socket joint, it is done. In cold weather, you may experience difficulties in getting the bird done. If so, finish cooking in an oven preheated to 300 degrees, being careful not to over-cook.

One of the advantages of smoked fowl, is that you can eat what you want, then take the remaining pieces and wrap it in saran wrap or plastic bags and freeze it. It will last for about 7 months. After thawing, the meat can be flaked from the bone. It makes excellent sandwiches, soups, salads or other snacks.

FAST SMOKE CHICKEN OR TURKEY

Take pre-cooked chicken or turkey, de-bone it, and place meat in a greased bake dish. Place in smoker for one hour, remove and serve. Makes excellent sandwiches, casseroles, gravies or salads.

SMOKED NUTS

You may take any type of nuts — peanuts, cashews, wal-nuts, almonds, etc., and give them a smoked flavor that is out of this world. Get a light stainless or nylon screen to hold the nuts and let the smoke through. Spread the screen across one of your smoker's racks and you are in business.

SMOKED CHEESE

There is almost no end to the number of things that can take a smoke flavor, often improving the taste immeasurably. Smoked cheese is one example. Try various cheeses but swiss cheese is a good one to start with. Using a baking cup or dish that cheese can mold into without spilling over the edge. Smoke the cheese for 1½ hours, remove and allow to cool, then refrigerate. Once cooled it can be removed from the dish and served. It should be kept refrigerated.

SMOKED HOT DOGS and VIENNA SAUSAGE

Talk about hors d' oeuvres, you can walk from here to Moscow and you won't find better ones anywhere than this. Place the weiners in the smoker for one hour. Remove to serving tray. Slice them crossways, about ¼ to ½ inch thick and put a toothpick in each. For a little class, serve with a spicy sauce.

SMOKED BACON, HAM or OTHER PORK

The meat should be soaked in a standard brine mixture — 1 quart water, ½ cup salt and a ½ cup sugar for about 2 to 4 hours. (The thicker the cut of meat, the longer it should stay in the brine. It should then be in the smoker from 2 to 4 hours, again depending on the thickness. Most any pork product with a smoke flavor is a real treat.

SMOKED GLAZED HAM

Here is a product that you won't find at the supermarket's meat counter or in a butcher shop. It is a real treat that will be a pleasant surprise to friends. Be sure to try it.

Take a precooked ham and remove all outside skin. Score the ham fat with a sharp knife by making diamond cutting criss cross parallel lines one-fourth inch deep. Then rub the following mixture on the outside of the ham.

1 cup curing salt — 1 cup brown sugar
Add a few cloves if you wish

Place the ham in your smoker and smoke for four hours. After the smoking period is completed, remove and cool. The ham should then be wrapped and placed in the refrigerator to later be prepared with your favorite ham recipe.

HICKORY SMOKED BEEF CHUNKS

Place the beef chunks in a standard brine for 2 to 4 hours, depending on size. Wash them off, dry for one hour, then into the smoker for 2 to 4 hours. Now cut into small sections and serve.

P.S. If you are a beer lover, you'll be hard pressed to come up with a better combination than hickory smoked beef chunks along with your glass of brew.

BEANS FIT FOR A KING

How about some smoked beans. Fix a casserole of your favorite pork and beans in a baking dish. Place the dish in your smoker for three hours and stir the beans occasionally. Remove from the smoker, then finish the dish in a preheated oven at 350 degrees for one hour.

Another method I've used with happy results is to smoke a couple of pork chops until done, then shread them into a baking dish filled with Campbell's Pork and Beans (or equivalent). Add a little smoked flavored barbeque sauce and mix well, then into the oven until piping hot. Goes extremely well with all barbecued meats. Be sure to try it at your next barbecue.

SMOKE PORK

There are a number of items that can be prepared quickly and easily in your smoker. Any of the following items will take on a delightful hickory smoke flavor if placed in your smoker for about 25 minutes.

Frankfurters	**Pork Roast**
Link Sausage	**Pork Chops**
Bacon	**Spareribs**

With a little imagination, your smoker will open up many new dishes. Consider smoked spareribs and sauerkraut, smoked ham and scalloped potatoes. smoked pork roast, etc.

CHAPTER 20
OLD FASHIONED JERKY

Daniel Boone, Davy Crockett and many of our other pioneers would have had a tough time had it not been for smoked jerky. It was one of their primary everday foods. As of this writing, jerky commands around $12.00 per pound at the grocery. It would have to be good to command those kind of prices and it is. The pioneers, of course, make their jerky from buffalo or venison. Those two items are hard to come by nowadays but you can still make excellent mouth-watering beef jerky in your back yard. The recipe that follows not only makes superb beef jerky but is also excellent for deer, elk, moose, etc.

Here is one of the advantages of making jerky — you don't need a high priced cut piece of meat. In fact, it seems the poorer the cut of meat, the better the jerky becomes. But, no matter whether you use low cost or high cost cuts of meat, the result will be the same, a delicious tasting product. You will find that round steak is excellent for making jerky.

In preparing your jerky for smoking, it is very important that you slice the meat with the grain. Do not cut against the grain as you might normally do. You should start out with a very sharp knife. First, cut off all the fat. Fat gives the jerky a rancid taste as it spoils rather easily.

Slice the meat about one-half inch thick and approximately four inches wide and from six to twelve inches long. If you partially freeze the meat, it is usually easier to cut. Below is the brine mix for jerky.

BRINE FOR JERKY
2 quarts of water   **½ cup sugar**
1 cup curing salt   **4 tablespoon black pepper**

Place strips of meat in a non-aluminum container. If they are crowded, double the above brine solution. A weighted plate may be placed on the meat to make certain that all portions of the meat are completely submerged. You should cure the meat in the brine for eight to ten hours.

After the brining period is over, remove the strips of meat, and wash each piece thoroughly under cold running tap water. Remove excess moisture with paper towels or cloth and allow to air dry for 60 minutes.

After the air drying is complete, rub the meat with a seasoning of your choice such as garlic salt, onion salt, pepper, etc. Now place the meat in your smoker.

Smoking time in the smoker is from nine to twelve hours. You can tell when jerky is done when it becomes stiff like a twisted rope. However, a quick check can be made by breaking open a piece to check the center. It should then be removed from the smoker, allowed to cool, then it should be kept in the refrigerator.

CHAPTER 21
HOW TO SMOKE VENISON

Smoked venison is a delightful treat. After your next deer hunt, assuming it was successful, try your hand at the following techniques for preparing venison.

5 — 10 pounds of	**Molasses**
lean deer meat	**Vinegar**
Brown Sugar	**Salt and Pepper**

Cut the meat into strips about 6 to 8 inches long, about 1 to 2 inches wide and not more than ½ inch thick.

Make a brine solution by combining a quantity of salt, vinegar and water in a crock or deep bowl. Soak the meat overnight in the solution.

In a spearate bowl, mix 1 cup of salt and ½ cup of brown sugar. Remove the meat from the brine solution after overnight soaking and dredge the meat in the salt and brown sugar rubbing it well into the meat. Now rub a ½ teaspoon of molasses on each strip of meat, then roll the entire quantity of meat in a piece of clean cloth and store in a cool place for 4 to 5 hours.

After proper time has elasped, remove the meat and rinse off under cold running water. You need to rinse thoroughly or meat will be too salty. Next, dry each piece with paper towels, then sprinkle black pepper sparingly on the strips. The meat is now ready to smoke. If you wish, you may again rub a small amount of molasses and brown sugar into the meat. It will give the meat a sweeter taste after the smoking.

Now place the meat in your smoker. It requires about 5 to 8 hours of smoking, depending on your preference for doneness.

The wood chips used for smoking should be either hickory, hard maple, apple or cherry.

After you have tried the above technique, you may find the meat is too salty for your particular taste. It simply means the meat wasn't rinsed long enough. On future efforts, after the brine cure, soak the meat in cold water for about one hour, then rinse and proceed.

May I close by wishing you good luck, good fishing and good eating.